Rediscovering Hemingway in Bangladesh and India, 1971–2006

Rabiul Hasan

University Press of America,® Inc.
Lanham · Boulder · New York · Toronto · Plymouth, UK

Library of Congress Control Number: 2010929165
ISBN: 978-0-7618-5154-7 (paperback : alk. paper)
eISBN: 978-0-7618-5155-4

For my late father, Serajul Haque Mollah,
and my late mother, Mosammat Halima Khatoon

Contents

Epigraph   vii

Preface   ix

Acknowledgments   xi

Introduction   xiii

Chapter One: Teaching American Literature in Bangladesh and India   1

Chapter Two: Hemingway's Legend in Bangladesh and India   11

Chapter Three: Hemingway's Short Stories in Bangladesh   19

Chapter Four: Hemingway's Short Stories in India   31

Chapter Five: Hemingway's Novels in Bangladesh   47

Chapter Six: Hemingway's Novels in India   67

Conclusion   97

Notes   101

Bibliography   111

Index   115

About the Author   119

Twelve months, thirteen celebrations.

—Bengali Proverb

Preface

Of all the American authors that have been favorably received in Bangladesh and India, Ernest Hemingway (1899–1961) tops the list. This book examines the teaching and reception of Ernest Hemingway's works by scholars in academia in Bangladesh and India from 1971 to 2006, along with Hemingway's reception in Bangladeshi books, periodicals, and newspapers from that period.

Growing up in what was then East Pakistan in the period following its decolonization from Britain, I first encountered Hemingway's works as a high school student. Reading Hemingway in English and in translation, I found him to be an enigma, both in his lifestyle and in his ability to speak directly to me as a reader from afar. So intrigued was I by the man and his writing that even before emigrating to the United States to further my education, I translated four of his short stories into Bengali, my native language. Later, his influence on me as a poet was expansive: Hemingway—the man and the author—not only defied insularity, but also demonstrated that it was possible to write about everyday people who spoke in their own idiom.

During my formative years in what is now Bangladesh, I experienced not only the gradual transition from British influence on everyday life, but also the instability of the civil war between East and West Pakistan, which resulted in East Pakistan becoming the independent state of Bangladesh in 1971. These political and cultural clashes made me acutely aware not only of how social, political and cultural differences may filter the experience of reading literature, but also how they color the way of thinking of critics who influence our views of literature.

The aim of this book is to contribute to the limited and selected body of criticism of Hemingway in Bangladesh. Insofar as this book demonstrates the vitality of Hemingway's works for Bangladeshi readers today, it does so in part by challenging the insularity of British literary critics who were contemporaries of Hemingway; by questioning literary criticism across cultures with a colonial legacy; and by raising questions about the relevance of teaching American literature during periods of institutional transition in view of the debate over American studies programs in the aftermath of September 11, 2001.

In attempting to overcome some of the cross-cultural barriers inherent in a study of Hemingway's influence upon readers in the Indian sub-continent, this book reflects my intellectual journey to discover the cultural and institutional factors that filter the experience of reading Hemingway in Bangladesh and India today, and to respond to critics who ask if Hemingway's writing is still relevant after the turn of events of September 11, 2001. This study required me to retrace my own journey and return to Bangladesh and India in 2004 and 2005 to interview readers and critics directly and to obtain and examine relevant sources published in Bengali.

I commence my account of this journey by critically examining notable British and American perspectives of Hemingway's work found in Western publications. Next, relying on relevant Bangladeshi sources, including books, periodicals, and newspapers, published from 1971 to 2006, I give specific attention to the challenges of teaching of American literature in Bangladesh and India today, and the analyses and interpretations of Hemingway's short stories and novels that have been translated into Bengali. Finally, I examine Hemingway's reception in Bangladesh and India by his readers and "critics" used here in a generic sense: that is, the Hemingway scholars, students, and university and college faculty members with an interest in Hemingway; local authors who write in their native language, Bengali; the translators of Hemingway's novels and short stories; and general readers. Thus, we can examine the Hemingway legend in Bangladesh and India in the context of the teaching and reception of American literature in Bangladesh and India after 1971, and on its own terms. Would Hemingway have wanted anything less of us today?

Rabiul Hasan
Southern University
Department of English
Baton Rouge, Louisiana
January 2010

Acknowledgments

This book had its inception as a doctoral dissertation at Texas Tech University, where I received the friendship, encouragement and scholarly advice of many people. I take this opportunity to express my heartfelt appreciation, admiration and gratitude to Bryce D. Conrad, PhD, for his unfailing support and constant guidance during my graduate studies at Texas Tech. Indeed, without Professor Conrad's timely advice, first-rate expertise and unceasing inspiration, this study would have been impossible. I thank him for his understanding, patience, kindness and help. I also extend my sincere thanks and deepest gratitude to Michael K. Scoenecke, PhD, and John William Samson, PhD, for their cooperation, valuable suggestions and guidance of this work. My colleagues at Texas Tech University, as well as the ever-smiling and friendly staff of the Department of English, made my stay at Texas Tech a pleasant one, and I thank them for their friendship and encouragement. Thanks are also due to my colleague and friend in the English department at Southern University, Professor Thomas Morgan, for his confidence in my work.

The cooperation of many individuals and institutions in Bangladesh and India were essential to this study, and I wish to thank the individuals who granted interviews for their generosity of time and interest in meeting with me, their openness in sharing their views on Hemingway, and their professional insights and criticisms. I also wish to acknowledge Jadavpur University, Kolkata, West Bengal, India, and the Indo-American Centre for International Studies, Osmania University, Hyderadad, India, for facilitating my research in India.

My brother A. Z. M. Arif Hasan, MBBS, PhD, and my brother-in-law Shariful Islam, MBBS, also helped and supported me in many ways, which I deeply appreciate and recognize. Along with my other brothers and sisters, they have always believed in me and in my potential to accomplish my goals.

Finally, next to, of course, God, I express my appreciation and gratitude to my parents—my late father, Serajul Haque Mollah, and my late mother, Mosammat Halima Khatoon—for their unselfish and unfailing love and affection, unceasing inspiration and monumental sacrifices in helping me cross the River Jordan into this promised land. I would not have made it without them, the greatest of the great parents of the world. I owe them everything I am—now and forever.

Introduction

To evaluate the reception of Ernest Hemingway's works in Bangladesh and India, it is appropriate that we begin by gauging the appreciation of Hemingway in England. Why link the reception of Hemingway in Bangladesh and India with his appreciation in England? For historical reasons, educated readers and academics in the colonial Indian sub-continent first came into contact with Hemingway and his writings by way of British critics and authors. After 1947, the critique of the colonial legacy in the aftermath of British rule provided a point of departure for a revised assessment of Hemingway's works by educated readers in India and, later, Bangladesh.

Although scholars and academics in colonial India may have initially viewed Hemingway as a novelty, both as a man and as an author, many British critics in the 1930s and 1940s relegated Hemingway's literary importance to that of "a story-teller and particularly as a teller of war-stories."[1] As D. S. R. Welland put it, "His narrative powers and his dialogue have been admired, but the evaluation of their importance has been less easy to agree upon. . . . His powerful simplifications looked more salutary in some lights than in others."[2] The novelist and critic Wyndham Lewis provided an example of this type of qualified assessment in *Blasting and Bombardiering*, published in 1937: "Every Anglo-Saxon community should have its Hemingway to disinfect it of its inveterate 'uplift,' and provide a background of insensitiveness and alertness. . . . And then, of course, you need something else to dekiplingize you afterwards of your Hemingway."[3]

Insofar as these British critics later became victims of their own limited judgments of Hemingway, such criticisms were attributed to Hemingway's "achievement to date, coupled with the belief in his power to achieve maturity in a latter work."[4] Some even argued that if Hemingway had been personally known in England, his critics would have formed more favorable (and less snobbish) judgments of his writing. Welland, for example, believed that the Hemingway myth "suffered" in England "because it always reached the reader at second- or even third-hand."[5]

This particular critique of Hemingway may have been true in England, but not in colonial India, where Hemingway's reputation remained intact and unabashed. Hemingway's remoteness or lack of personal connection with his readers—not having traveled to colonial India or post-colonial Bangladesh or India, and not having acquainted himself with the people of these countries—did not lessen his popularity with them any more than it may have aggravated his myth. Instead, with the advent of the study of American literature in the British universities and colleges, Hemingway came to be recognized and studied with zeal and intensity on his own literary merits, not as an indication of his impact on English—that is, British—literature.

Still, according to Welland, it may be easier to detect the ups and downs of Hemingway's reputation than to fathom the extent of his influence:

> Any attempt at charting it in even the most general terms must begin by distinguishing between influence and imitation. The shoals of imitators of the Hemingway style, justifiably deplored by so many reviewers, have been less influenced, in any meaningful and constructive way, than many writers whose styles bear no superficial traces of Hemingwayese at all. There are hardly any major English novelists to whose work one may confidently point and say 'Here and here is the influence of Hemingway', and yet it is incontrovertible that the English novel would have developed differently had he not written.[6]

Philip Henderson was more direct and less equivocal when he said that Hemingway "writes with a freshness and vitality unknown to the English novel."[7] Indeed, it was this quality of Hemingway's writing that helped him gain many of his British admirers, for Hemingway empathized with all types of readers, young and old, unlike the English novelists. Writing on "Defects of English Novels" in 1935, Cyril Connolly argued that

> the English novelist never establishes a respect-worthy relationship with his reader. The American novelists, Hemingway, Hammett, Faulkner, Fitzgerald, O'Hara, for instance, write instinctively for men of their own age, men who enjoy the same things; . . . it is an intimacy which at its worst degenerates into dogginess, but which in general brings out everything that is natural, easy and unrepressed in the author. . . . English novels seem always to be written for superiors or inferiors, older or younger people, or for the opposite sex.[8]

Thus, despite claims that Hemingway was not a direct influence on modern English novelists, Hemingway's close identification with his subjects awakened his reviewers and readers to a mode of writing not found in English novels.

Subtle changes in the matrix distinguishing Hemingway's "influence and imitation" were forthcoming in 1938. Connolly found a resemblance between Hemingway's sentence patterns in *To Have and Have Not* (1937) and Christopher Isherwood's *Sally Bowles* (1937) and George Orwell's *Road to Wigan Pier* (1937). Connolly did not go so far as to label them an "influence;" he recognized them as a halfway improvement, but an improvement nonetheless. He was not yet generous enough to credit Hemingway with having an "influence" on English novelists of the caliber of Isherwood and Orwell.

Yet not everyone agreed with Connolly that Hemingway was having a measure of influence on English writing of the 1930s and 1940s. E. M. Forster, in 1944, while on a lecture tour on "English Prose between 1918 and 1939," dismissed Hemingway as an author who introduced "a new technique of conversation." Julian Symons, however, saw things in a different light. Symons sidetracked Graham Greene, Evelyn Waugh and Christopher Isherwood as typical of the era and found in their work "the shadowing presence of Ernest Hemingway." But even Symons hastened to add the influences of Franz Kafka and Aldous Huxley on Greene, and the mass media on all of these authors. Thus, the influence of Hemingway on English authors may have dwindled; but, to his readers, Hemingway has remained an historic figure, if not a living force.

In a review of *For Whom the Bell Tolls* in 1941, V. S. Pritchett best summed up Hemingway as an historic figure:

> No other prose writer since Lawrence has had his influence. It lies partly in his manner of writing, which is a sort of stylization of vernacular speech, but chiefly in his view of life and character. More than any other writer he has defined for us the personality of our own time. . . . I rather think we have to go as far back as Byron and Byronism before we can find a type which has been stamped as vividly as Hemingway's upon a decade. . . . What has attracted us to the Hemingway man is his adaptability, the lightness of his luggage, his mobility. . . . The Hemingway man has become an expert in de-civilization. We admire him because he has made terms with his time.[9]

Pritchett's assertions lead us to ask, Did India's knowledge of Hemingway's writing come only through percolation by way of English aesthetics? If colonial India came to know about Hemingway's reputation second-hand, via England, how did this change after 1947? And how far did Hemingway the man go in "de-civilizing" England's colonial possession of the Indian sub-continent?

The answers to these questions are intertwined with the history of British rule and the teaching of literature in Bangladesh and India. On the one hand, scholars and educated readers were already familiar with Hemingway's work when British influences gave way in India.—India, along with Pakistan, became independent of British rule in 1947. Pakistan, consisting of East and West Pakistan, further split in two. In 1971, after a bloody civil war, what was formerly East Pakistan became Bangladesh, an independent country.—On the other hand, with the resultant separation from British authority came greater identification with world literatures.

Although the introduction of American literature into the English curricula was moderately slow in Bangladesh and India, its subject matter and scope have always fascinated the reading public and attracted considerable attention from literary critics and scholars. In both Bangladesh and India, the reception of American literature intensified with the success of a number of American novelists in evincing a discernable influence beyond America, especially in Europe. Indeed, awarding the Nobel Prize in literature to a number of twentieth century American authors, including Hemingway in 1954, undeniably brought the reading public, professional critics, and scholars in Bangladesh and India much closer to an understanding and appreciation of the culture, society, and people of a country from which they were separated geographically by a distance of more than ten thousand miles.

Despite vast geographical distances as well as complex cultural, political and socio-economic differences, religious influences, logistical problems, language barriers, and the paucity of relevant sources, this book examines the Hemingway legend and his works in the context of the teaching and reading of American literature in Bangladesh and India after 1971.

Chapter One:
Teaching American Literature in
Bangladesh and India

A discussion of American authors and the teaching of American literature in Bangladesh and India calls for some historical background. Our understanding of an American author such as Ernest Hemingway in this context does so even more. This discussion takes as it starting point the introduction of English literature in India during the nineteenth century, when it was under British rule.

A Colonial Mission

Ostensibly to educate native Indians, the British, through the Charter Act of 1813, began teaching English literature in India in the early nineteenth century. The teaching of English literature, however, was duplicitous in that it masked an ulterior motive. By introducing English literary texts into the curricula of Indian educational institutions, the British sought—with discernable success—to create a class of subjects who were sympathetic to the royal cause. Syed Manzoorul Islam notes that the teaching of English literature was designed to cover the stains of colonialism:

> English literature texts, with their refined aesthetics and values embedded in them, were expected to create and perpetuate a myth of superior race and civilization. The colonizers in the process of the propagation of the myth and the values would be absolved of their brutality and violence on the ground that they were indeed on a civilizing mission.[1]

S. M. Islam goes on to note that Lord Macaulay defined the make-up of the class of subalterns in colonialistically unambiguous terms: "Indian in blood and colour, but English in taste, in opinions, in morals, and in intellect."[2] As a result of the British colonial legacy, almost all of the universities and colleges in India, and later Bangladesh, taught mostly British literature until the later part of the twentieth century.

The Rise of Modernism

By comparison, the introduction of American literature in India and Bangladesh seemed almost accidental. According to S. M. Islam, "American literature was first introduced in Bangladesh"—then Bengal—"in the 1940s when a couple of American authors were included in the Masters Degree curriculum of the English department of Dhaka University."[3] As S. M. Islam explains,

> This altering of course was more marginal than substantive, for this was a time when literature departments were rushing to incorporate modern literature in their course contents, as post-Rabindranath Tagore poets of the thirties and fiction writers writing under the influence of authors such as Joyce and Wolfe were creating a distinct body of modernist literature in the Bengali, and profoundly influencing literary tastes of the reading public, including professors and deans.[4]

Ironically, to quench an ever-increasing thirst of students for American literature, only a few American authors who were considered precursors of American modernism—namely, Walt Whitman, Herman Melville and Mark Twain—were permitted to be taught. Hence, the place of American authors remained uncertain as works by British authors continued to dominate the syllabi.

This preponderance of British literature in the curricula of English departments of the universities and colleges throughout India remained unchanged, especially in Bangladesh (then East Pakistan). Even after Bangladesh seceded from Pakistan on December 16, 1971, the English curricula throughout Bangladesh remained virtually British during the 1970s. This scenario changed and took a giant step forward only when the University of Dhaka, along with a few other public and private universities, consistently began to offer courses in American literature in the 1980s. Students and faculty alike spontaneously and wholeheartedly welcomed this long-awaited incorporation of American literature into the English curricula. Needless to say, the interest in American literature in college and university campuses has increased greatly since the 1980s. Consequently, with the establishment of increasing numbers of private and parochial colleges and universities, there has been a growing "demand for a separate American literature paper and more authors and texts were added."[5]

Although many factors contributed to this increasing emphasis on American literature in the English curricula, three are worth mentioning. First, the U.S. Information Service (USIS) had "set up well stocked and open shelf libraries in a number of towns of Bangladesh, which were patronized by large numbers of readers. These libraries acquainted whole sections of readers with American writers—famous as well as not so-famous." Second, "scholarship and fellowship schemes of the American government (such as the Fulbright fellowship) encouraged Bangladeshi scholars and academics to go for higher studies in the U.S., and quite a few chose to read American literature. They came back with fresh ideas about both expansion of the syllabus, and improvement of pedagogical practices." Third, "poets and fiction writers were commissioned by USIS and local publishers to translate major American authors into the

Bengali."[6] Thus, translations provided one of the most important ways the general readership—many of whom were weak in comprehending the English language—came in contact with American literature. As the quality of education improved, readers moved from reading translations to original texts. The observations above also applied to equally Indian scholars and academics.

In addition, among the most significant catalysts of the Hemingway legend in Bangladesh and India were film adaptations of his novels and short stories. These English-language films were accessible to English-speaking viewers; and being movie buffs, educated men and women thronged the theaters since the1950s each time a Hemingway film was released. Theaters were full the first few weeks, to be followed by a modest crowd thereafter. In addition to the theaters, billboards in certain parts of Dhaka and Kolkata (formerly Calcutta), were instrumental in jump-starting the appetite of the moviegoers. Through these billboards, Bangladeshi and Indian readers could connect America's best known film stars with characters from Hemingway's fiction: Humphrey Bogart in *To Have and Have Not*; Spencer Tracy as Santiago in *The Old Man and the Sea*; Rock Hudson as Fredric Henry in *A Farewell to Arms*; Tyrone Power and Ava Gardner as Jake and Brett in *The Sun Also Rises*; Burt Lancaster or Lee Marvin and Ronald Reagan in *The Killers*; Gregory Peck and Susan Hayward in *The Snows of Kilimanjaro*; and Gary Cooper and Ingrid Bergman in *For Whom the Bell Tolls*. These film adaptations of Hemingway's novels did not compete with or diminish his readership in Bangladesh and India; on the contrary, they spurred it, helping to make his literary works all the more popular and enduring.

Teaching American Literature

Many of these early readers became English majors at public and private universities, taking courses in 19th- and 20th-century American literature. Some went on to take survey courses in early American literature that included authors such as Thomas Morton and William Bradford. Today, the University of Chittagong, a leading public university in Bangladesh, offers a second-year honors course that showcases authors ranging from Anne Bradstreet to Cotton Mather to Michel Crevecoeur. Private universities have followed suit. Most of them now offer several courses on modern and contemporary American authors, in addition to survey courses in early American literature. The following informal survey of American literature courses at leading universities in Bangladesh finds that, despite a lingering emphasis on British authors, among the various courses featuring works by modern and contemporary American authors, Hemingway is consistently represented.

BRAC University, a private school funded by a non-governmental organization, in its British-laden syllabus for the undergraduate program in English, offers two survey courses in American literature: ENG 354: Survey of American Literature I; and ENG 355: Survey of American Literature II. The first showcases authors such as Bradstreet, Taylor, Franklin, Poe, Hawthorne,

Melville, Emerson, Thoreau, and Whitman. The second showcases authors such as Dickinson, Twain, Chopin, O'Neill, Frost, Hemingway, Fitzgerald, Miller, Lowell, Bellow, and Morrison. On the modern and contemporary side, this university offers ENG 319, a course with a long list of British authors. The only American modernists included are Williams, Stevens, Pound, and Eliot. Hence, British authors continue to be more frequently represented, if not over represented, in courses on modern literature.

Similarly, at East West University in Bangladesh, the offerings in American literature are limited. East West offers only two American literature courses for its undergraduate English majors, representing authors from Hawthorne to Hemingway. The two courses are ENG 420: American Literature (1620–1891); and ENG 426: American Literature (Modern to Contemporary). Aside from the arbitrary selection of dates—1620–1891—ENG 420 includes authors such as Hawthorne, Melville, Longfellow, Thoreau, James, Twain, and Whitman. ENG 426 includes modernists such as Dickinson, Frost, O'Neill, and, of course, Hemingway.

North South University (NSU), the oldest private university in Bangladesh, offers its undergraduate English majors only two traditional yet appreciatory courses in American literature: ENG 327: Survey of American Literature; and ENG 328: Masterworks of American Literature. ENG 327 introduces the "works of representative American writers from the 17th century to the present;" and ENG 328 deals with a "selection of major works in verse, drama, and prose from American literature from the 17th century to the present."[7] Given their broad scope, these two courses could serve as a springboard for well-ramified and distinctive future American literature courses at NSU.

Comparable American literature courses—two in all—are included in the syllabus of the Master of Arts in Literature program at the University of Dhaka, Bangladesh's oldest and most prestigious public university: ENG 507: American Literature I (From Bradford to Twain); and ENG 508: American Literature II (From James to Morrison). According to the syllabus, students in ENG 507 will "study the major writers from the Puritan period to the period immediately after the Civil War;" and "students will be expected to know the historical and ideological backgrounds in which these writers and their writings were situated." Authors to be studied are Bradford, Bradstreet, Taylor, Crevecoeur, Poe, Hawthorne, Melville, Douglass, Whitman, Dickinson, and Twain. American Literature II, in addition to dealing with "major poets and novelists of the 20th century, will study the major dramatists of the period. Students will be expected to know the social and historical context of these writers and their writings." Authors to be read are James, Hemingway, Fitzgerald, O'Neill, Tennessee Williams, Miller, Frost, William Carlos Williams, Rich, Bellow, and Morrison.[8]

A Dearth of Instructors

One discernable feature of these syllabi is the absence of a single-author, American literature course. A number of variables work toward this end. First, public colleges and universities in Bangladesh and India lack sufficient resources, that is, funds, to add new classes that require them to hire additional instructors. Reflecting the economy of a country with one of the lowest per capita incomes in the world, universities in Bangladesh, followed by India, cannot yet afford this extra financial burden, despite the intrinsic and long-term benefits. Second, public colleges and universities lack instructors who are qualified to teach American literature survey courses, much less a single-author course.

The explanation for this dearth of instructors in American literature rests largely with the post-graduate educational system in countries that are part of the British Commonwealth, which still perpetuates the colonial legacy. As members of the British Commonwealth, and with scholarships from the British government—known generally as the Commonwealth Scholarship—Bangladesh and India send their top-notch, cream-of-the-crop graduates to other Commonwealth countries, such as Canada, Australia, New Zealand, and of course, Great Britain, for higher education. As a result, these graduates with terminal degrees are well trained to teach British literature, but not American literature. When they return home to teach, they logically become comfortable teaching British literature; and if they have to teach American literature courses, they do it strictly as a matter of academic responsibility, not as it should be. Ironically, the prospect of offering a single-author, American literature course is further relegated to an uncertain future, thus depriving students the opportunity to attain valuable and indispensable knowledge.

In addition, the academic committee designated to oversee the formulation and execution of the syllabus plays a crucial role. Here, again, the training and preferences of committee members have a great deal to do with the exclusion of a single-author American literature course. Perhaps the entrenched mentality of the key personnel will shift as the demand for more period-literature courses and more single-author literature courses grows among the budding population of students craving a taste for American literature.

The Movement for American Studies

Despite these institutional factors, English departments in universities in Bangladesh and India are aware of the efficacy of having a well-blended syllabus of English and American literature courses. In fact, a movement is underway among a group of dedicated faculty, albeit a resilient and vocal minority, to expand the existing syllabi, because "American literature was, and is still being taught by these departments."[9]

This nascent movement appears to be moving in a positive direction. If morning shows the day—to use a Bengali expression—the University of Dhaka in Bangladesh expects to have an Institute of American Studies in the future, to be followed by a separate department of American literature. And if the University of Dhaka realizes an Institute of American Studies and a separate department of American literature, then the founding of the Bangladesh Association for American Studies (BAAS) in 1986 was a ground for this reality.

In an interview Golam Sarwar Chowdhury, professor and chairman of the English department at the University of Chittagong, who was instrumental in the founding of the BAAS, reflected on the organization. When asked about the importance of an academic program in American studies for a poor country like Bangladesh that needs to improve the standard of living of its people, Chowdhury stated that

> American studies could work as a conduit that could bring in ideas and thoughts from the U.S. and the West that are absolutely essential for strengthening important institutions in Bangladesh. If the country can't continue to go on the democratic way, development of its economy will become extremely difficult. American studies is an academic discipline that doesn't just teach about the U.S. It also helps in broadening the understanding of ideas related to a democratic and secular society.[10]

The Debate over American Studies after 9/11

Increasingly, religious fundamentalism presents a challenge to ideas related to a democratic and secular society. Arguing from an American studies point of view, G. S. Chowdhury views the rise of religious fundamentalism in the United States from an historical point of view:

> The U.S. was a country founded by the early pilgrims who saw the land as a 'city atop the hill.' The newly discovered land promised unrestricted religious freedom for the puritans who crossed the Atlantic following religious persecution in England. From then onwards, religion remained a strong factor in American culture. Consider the sermons of Cotton Mather and his peers. They all spoke about an angry God and threatened hellfire to those who didn't abide by God's law. This strong religious spirit still remains internalized in American society.[11]

An understanding then of how freedom of religion enhances the potential of democracy may be of assistance to democratic institutions and the culture of Bangladesh.

Chowdhury, however, fails to distinguish between the Puritan (one of many varieties of Christianity) roots of the foundation of the United States and the arbitrary imposition of religion as the only guiding light of the Constitution that moves the apparatus of the government. The United States was founded to practice religion any way one chooses as long as it does not encroach upon others' faith and belief systems. Actually, the U.S. government is a secular one as has been the case since the administration of George Washington, who, in turn, believed the Constitution to be a secular document. In view of the 9/11 tragedy, Chowdhury, however, regrets what he views as the regeneration of the Puritan "religious spirit" and its fullest execution by the George W. Bush administration to "police the rest of the world."[12] He calls this type of "tendency" by America as "belligerent" and says it is conducted as a "secular version" of the same religious value that made the early pilgrims think of themselves as the chosen people destined to show light to an otherwise benighted world."[13]

G. S. Chowdhury goes on to say that in Bangladesh, "American studies, however, is entirely secular, and questions the hegemonic role of the U.S. in terms of its relationship with the rest of the world."[14] Needless to say, the American studies program in India is also entirely secular.

Chowdhury is again wrong here on a number of observations. First, it is naïve to assume that there is a byproduct of foreign policy, such as a "secular version" of a religion, whether it is Christianity or Islam. In Bangladesh, India, as well as in the United States, the faith in, and practice of, a religion is considered a personal matter. As a result, secularism as embedded in the U.S. Constitution, not a "secular version" of Christianity, plays a cardinal role in the formulation and execution of American foreign policy. The United States of America has never put on the façade of being called the "Christian Republic of America" in the way that many Muslim nations in the Middle East are officially declared "Islamic." Many of these nations govern themselves according to their religious beliefs and practices, often through the application of literal meanings of God's commandments. If the United States has a "secular" religious twist to its formulation and execution of its foreign policy, as Chowdhury willfully or mistakenly claims, it is foremost guided by the consideration of national security after the 9/11 attack.

In secular and democratic America, unlike countries in the Middle East, both secular and religious voices are tolerated and recognized. In the United States, one can look at things from different points of view—religious or secular—and express these viewpoints in an appropriate journal, whether it is a mouthpiece for an American studies program in a college or university or in everyday life. Second, it is cynical and hypocritical to suggest that because American studies programs are often funded by grants from federal agencies such as the National Endowment for the Humanities (NEH), they cannot maintain their objectivity. This is untrue and a virulent distortion of facts, and at best propaganda. It is, however, amazing—and ironic—that Chowdhury acknowledges, appreciates and supports funding of the research and teaching of American studies in Bangladesh and India by the U.S. government, but at the same time believes that it might not be "possible to have the proper perspective given the source of funding."[15] As Chowdhury states,

It's true that whatever is done with American studies in Bangladesh is done with the help of funding procured from the U.S. State Department. Yes, if meaningful research, study, and teaching of American studies are to continue in this discipline, we've (sic) to look for other sources of funding, because a continuous dependence on the American establishment is bound to affect the objectivity and neutrality of the research of American studies in Bangladesh or in South Asia.[16]

Surprisingly, a majority of the English faculty and the students—both undergraduate and graduate—do not subscribe to G. S. Chowdhury's arbitrary notion of the corrupting influence of funds from the U.S. government to oversee and bolster American studies programs in Bangladesh and India. As a matter of fact, they welcome and appreciate this "good samaritan" approach of financial aid by the Department of State. They firmly believe that without the U.S. government's direct monetary and moral support, American studies programs will not germinate and prosper in Bangladesh and India.

But the real problems about installing American studies programs, and more important, offering American literature courses lay elsewhere, not in the financial realm, as Chowdhury argues. According to S. M. Islam, the problems are cultural, political, and experiential: "Interpreting cultural, political and experiential aspects of texts has become a difficult exercise."[17] These problems point to the situation that many faculty members in the English departments in Bangladesh and India lack orientation, training, and degrees in American literature. As S. M. Islam notes, even faculty who teach American literature "had to take many classes simply to familiarize the students with terms and events like Puritanism, Transcendentalism and the Civil War."[18]

In addition, recent developments, such as the end of the Cold War, the emergence of the United States as the single superpower, the Gulf War, and the events of September 11, 2001 and their aftermath, are "raising new questions, interests, even suspicion, which American literature is expected to explain adequately. Multiculturalism, which is pushing a wide range of social expressions, values and practices into the center of our academic discourses, is posing questions of its own which also need to be answered."[19]

Although many faculty members in the English departments wrestle with these questions, they also groan "under the influence of critical cultural theories," and thus "question the reductive imperatives" of a monolithic culture. Until the 1980s, American literature courses reflected this bias of a monolithic culture as students were given a "limited range of choice of authors and texts . . . the selection appeared hierarchal, foundational, authoritative—and showed a lack of understanding of the issues being raised in the process." The selection of American authors was prompted by a monolithic racial vision, that is, by a bias for the major white writers. This bias and skewed selection process even bypassed Southern white writers. Black and women writers of considerable repute were also sidelined. What bias and subjectivity there was that marred the selection process was "more a matter of expediency than intention. Space was limited—therefore, it was not possible to include all."[20]

These challenges, new as they are, can be resolved. One way is to offer combined courses in American literature and film to complement each other, which some private universities have pursued and implemented. Nonetheless, the major mode of teaching consists of lectures and tutorials. To rouse interest and instill insight into American life, culture, and civilization—and thus to offset demands for regional, ethnic, and cultural courses—BRAC University in Bangladesh offers a course on The Global Village: Studies in Television, which has a broad American content. Similarly, East West University in Bangladesh has a cultural studies course that "sets the ground for further inquiry into any related field of study."[21]

Another way to upgrade American literature is to pay attention to what the students have to say about Americanism, and address their questions about cultural norms and values in America, the role of the family, immigration, leisure and so on, as they try to find answers to all these questions through satellite channels. Although it is true that films and television shows on these channels faithfully portray American life, society, and culture, most of these are written and produced by American scholars and professionals in the film industries. According to G. S. Chowdhury,

> A Bangladeshi student would find a discussion from his or her cultural perspective missing in these materials. Over the last 15 years, the Bangladesh Association for American Studies, which has a large representation from the English departments, has held a number of seminars on American life and culture. The publications of the proceedings such as *The American City, Family in America, Religion in America*, etc. provide a wide spectrum of Bangladeshi views."[22]

A Valued Tradition

Finally, one tradition has kept American literature alive in Bangladesh and India: the practice of translating important authors into Bengali. With new names added to the list each year, this valued tradition has been instrumental in keeping students, scholars, and non-scholastic readers alike posted about the contemporary developments in American literature. S. M. Islam, for example, has been working on an anthology of American literature for Asian students for a few years and says that it has

> taken into account Asian sensitivities and particular likings for particular authors. In an age of multiculturalism, particularly after September 11, local cultural sensitivities cannot be ignored while teaching literatures—whether English or American. In its insistence on a new understanding, the reality today is somewhat similar to the one after the de-colonization of South Asia. If this new understanding reflects the way today's youth view themselves, their society and culture, it will also influence the way American literature is taught in our universities in the coming days.[23]

As we shall see, reliable translations inescapably heighten students' interest and enlighten their minds about new authors and genres. In addition, definitive anthologies are boosted to successful pedagogies.

Chapter Two:
Hemingway's Legend
in Bangladesh and India

Today, it is more difficult than ever to gauge, assess, and evaluate Hemingway as a legend in Bangladesh and India, except through the minds of the reading public, students, college and university teachers, and amateur critics. A number of reasons account for this difficulty. First, unlike in the West, there is no systematic way in Bangladesh and India where one can conduct research to find out what was written on Hemingway in the past. Second, even if there is a clue about certain information or material, one cannot easily retrieve it. There is no retrieval system, such as an archive on Hemingway. Third, much of the critical writings on Hemingway that were published in earlier Bengali periodicals and newspapers in what was then East Pakistan, during the period of Pakistani rule (1947–71), were destroyed, misplaced, or lost forever during Bangladesh's liberation war (1971) against Pakistan. West Bengal, Bangladesh's western neighbor, and the Bengali-speaking provinces of India also lost a significant amount of critical writings on Hemingway before and after the independence of India from the British rule in 1947. Fourth, because of the lack of a systematic, organized, and central database, newspapers and periodicals were unable to store their information on Hemingway. Finally, publishers—because of lack of space—dispose of their newspapers and periodicals after an agreed on length of time.

Thus, researching Hemingway in Bangladesh and India presents challenges for researchers. In an attempt to compensate for the unavailability of previously published sources, I relied on oral history methods and conducted personal interviews of faculty and students at various public and private universities in Bangladesh and India during 2004 and 2005. The interviews were conducted in Bengali and English, according to the interviewee's preference, and were facilitated by use of a questionnaire that allowed for open-ended responses.

The Hemingway Mystique

The Hemingway legend in Bangladesh and India in the period after 1971 had its roots in an earlier American version of his legend. According to John A. Jones, "Critics have written about their own attitudes toward the legend rather than about their dispassionate critical interest in Hemingway's fiction,"[1] in part because Hemingway always camouflaged himself behind his impressive corpus of literary output in all genres. Thus, to introduce this discussion of the

Hemingway legend in Bangladesh and India in the period after 1971, we begin with a brief survey of how the Hemingway mystique had played out in America.

With the publication of Burton Rascoe's review of *In Our Time in Arts and Decorations* in 1925, the Hemingway legend slowly but gradually began to take root. Besides generalizing about Hemingway the novelist, Rascoe fine-tuned his other themes and concerns of life, masculinity, adventure, suffering and defeat, and violence and loss. Hemingway was no less instrumental in augmenting the legend in *Death in the Afternoon* (1932), where he chided Jean Cocteau, Aldous Huxley, and El Greco for being insincere, artificial, unmanly, and "fakers" in their productions.[2] Later, because of his virulent comments on Cocteau, Huxley, and El Greco, reviewer Max Eastman confronted him in the office of publisher-editor Maxwell Perkins on August 11, 1937, and thereupon a tough-guy image of Hemingway emerged.[3]

Prior to this, the appearance of Clifton Fadiman's article entitled, "Ernest Hemingway: An American Byron," in the January 18, 1933 issue of *Nation* gave rise to "the image of Hemingway as a democratic, proletarian Byron."[4] Representing this new brand of romanticism, Hemingway received more publicity and name-recognition than any other American author:

> Hemingway is the hero thrown up by the American ferment, as, in a different way on profounder level, D. H. Lawrence was thrown up by the industrial ferment of England. Hemingway is the modern primitive, who makes as fresh a start with the emotions as his forefathers did with the soil. He is the frontiersman of the loins, heart, and biceps, the stoic Red Indian minus traditions, scornful of the past, bare of sentimentality, catching the muscular life in a plain and muscular prose. He is the hero who distrusts heroism; he is the prophet of those who are without faith.[5]

Referring to the *lost generation*, Fadiman went to say that, like Byron, Hemingway was decidedly romantic, zeroing in on the postwar disillusion, turmoil, and bitterness: "Like Byron, he expresses the aspirations of that portion of his generation which genuinely feels itself lost and is eager to admire a way of life which combines lostness with courage and color."[6] Both share a sense of fatality, "the courting of violence, darkness, and even death," which "is a kind of splendid, often very beautiful, disease of the imagination noticeable during periods of social decay."[7]

Jones found that from 1933 to 1936, Hemingway's journalistic output of twenty-five pieces on hunting, fishing, and traveling, submitted to *Esquire*, with its largely male readership, further fueled the legend:

> Frequently, photographs of the author, smiling as he posed with a dead marlin, kudu, or lion, accompanied his articles. He always posed himself as a symbol of the masculine and healthful and the critics (or anybody he did not like) as symbols of the puerile and the abnormal.[8]

Hemingway's publications during the 1930s—*Death in the Afternoon*

(1932), *Green Hills of Africa* (1935), *To Have and Have Not* (1937), and *The Fifth Column* (1930)—all denoted "expressions of Hemingway the popular personality rather than Hemingway the artist."[9] Jones goes on to hypothesize that the poor reception of *Green Hills of Africa* in America

> must be attributed to Hemingway's attacks upon contemporary critics and writers, and to the widespread, unfavorable impression of the Hemingway legend on reviewers and critics, rather than to his avoidance of themes which critics thought important.[10]

Hemingway maintained his image during the 1940s. He wrote noticeably very little between 1941 and 1948, but managed to remain relentlessly in the news, either as a bearded hunter of German U-Boats or as a war correspondent and partisan in France. Malcolm Cowley, inspired by this macho image of Hemingway in the print media, wrote an article in the January 10, 1949 issue of *Life*, which was, as Jones puts it, "a heroic and flattering write up of Hemingway's personality and those of his habits and attitudes that were bound to be attractive to the public."[11] With the publication of *Across the River and into the Trees* in 1950, the perception of Hemingway the legend began to slacken; and by the time *The Old Man and the Sea* appeared in *Life* in 1952, it had mostly evaporated.[12]

The Man versus the Legend

The legend of Hemingway depicted in various American publications prospered and continued to grow in Bangladesh after it gained independence its 1971. To explore its dynamics there, we turn to the perspectives of teachers, readers and critics familiar with his literary work to help us understand how people of Bangladesh and India understand and identify with Hemingway.

The depiction of Hemingway as a legend over Hemingway as a man is not chronological or sequential; it is perceptive and symbolic. Tabassum Zaman, a faculty member in the Department of English at BRAC University, is unequivocal: "For me, Hemingway the legend overshadows Hemingway the man."[13] In contrast, Dr. Fakrul Alam, critic and professor of English at the University of Dhaka, looks at Hemingway from a shared reality: Hemingway as a man and as a legend form two sides of the same coin. This shared reality makes him more humane and down to earth. Alam states, "As a man, he seems to have learned to overcome his childhood traumas and put on the mask of the tough and yet sensitive man of perfection; the legendary Hemingway, of course, is the bullfighting, big game hunting, big fish-netting man."[14]

Hasan Al Zayed, a faculty member in the Department of English at East West University, disagrees. Al Zayed believes that Hemingway as a man and Hemingway as a legend are two different entities in the author's life:

> They belong to two different roles; two polarized persons by nature

and insight. The man, as I look at him and try to understand today, seems more introverted and less sure about his willingness and capability, at times very frustrated. The legend is that of a 'superman' or to be precise the 'James Bond' of literature.[15]

The image of Hemingway as a man, however, preceded the image of Hemingway as a legend among the readers, translators, publishers, students, and college and university teachers. Indeed, the images of Hemingway as a man and as a legend often overlap and are not necessarily mutually exclusive for Bangladeshi readers. As Dr. Rebecca Sultana, professor of English at East West University, states,

> I don't believe that a writer's personal life should influence my perspective of him or her. As a man, I believe Hemingway had such an inflated sense of self that it became hard to reconcile with the fact that he can become lesser than that. It affected his personal relationships and affected his prospect of life that he couldn't foresee anything less for the future and had to end his life prematurely. His violent death transformed him over time into a legend in Bangladesh, enhanced by newspaper and magazine articles and discussions sponsored and held by literary groups.[16]

Dr. Khaliquzzaman Elias, professor of English at North South University, has a similar train of thought. According to Elias,

> Legends, although grossly distorted, are built on reality. Since his death in 1961, media in Bangladesh has been laboring to reconstruct the exotic traits of Hemingway's life. This is fueled by the facts that Hemingway set background of his fiction in exotic locales such as Cuba, France, and Spain. Hemingway as a man was supersensitive and very complicated. It is said that when he got the Nobel Prize before him, he lost his composure and later sulked for many days. A very active, charismatic public figure, but at heart lonely— committing suicide—this is something complex."[17]

Tahmina Ahmed, a Hemingway scholar and associate professor of English at the University of Dhaka, weaves her own explanation: "I think Hemingway at first created a legend about himself and then later lived accordingly."[18] Dr. Showkat Hussain, professor of English at the University of Dhaka, agrees. According to Hussain, "The legend is perhaps bigger than the man and that is how it is usually."[19] Dr. Kaiser Haque, critic and professor of English at the University of Dhaka, concurs but with a different twist: "Hemingway the man is more complex and interesting than the legend.[20]" Shuchi Karim, who teaches English at BRAC University, hammers home the familiar yet personal point that

> he is more of a legend than a 'man.' It is very difficult to judge him as a 'man' because my knowledge is limited and also because it is almost impossible for any reader not to get biased while reading

Hemingway as his reputation as 'Hemingway' precedes his writing at times.[21]

Yet others emphasize with Hemingway as a man first and then as a legend. Critic, essayist and former chairman of the Department of English at the University of Dhaka, Dr. Sirajul Islam Chowdhury states that

> the man is greater than the legend around him. There were no pretensions in his life; he was what he was. He lived dangerously but wrote in a quiet manner, which signifies that within the man there was an artist. The artist was more powerful than the man.[22]

Chowdhury's assessment is echoed by journalist Khondker Ali Ashraf, an assistant editor of the Dhaka-based Bengali-language newspaper, *Dainik Jugantor*. According to Ashraf,

> When I read Hemingway—and I have read him a number of times—the images of him as a man first dawn on me rather than the images of him as a legend. His colorful and boisterous life in Spain, France, Italy as well as his manly quest and perilous adventure in Africa eventually catapulted him to a legend.[23]

Tahmina Zaman Godhuli, who was completing a Master of Arts degree in English at the University of Dhaka, has a political explanation for this dualism. According to Godhuli,

> The Hemingway legend emanates from Hemingway the individualist. He fought for individual freedom in the Spanish Civil War as well as in World War I. His African adventures as depicted in his novels also make him an individualist, paving the way for his superhuman status in the minds of readership in Bangladesh and India. Students adore him for his individual endurance against all odds and for putting on a macho image even in the face of inevitable failure and defeat.[24]

Zakeria Shirazii, critic, journalist and an assistant editor of the Bangladeshi English-language newspaper, *The Independent*, agrees: "In some persons there is a stirring emotion, an irrepressible urge for discovery called adventure. If we can imagine anyone as personification of adventure, then he is Ernest Hemingway."[25]

Finally, like many Bangladeshi and Indian observers of Hemingway, American expatriates in Bangladesh sing a similar tune. Carl Bloom, a graduate of the University of Southern Mississippi-Hattiesburg, and now a faculty member in the Department of English at North South University, states,

> As a legend, he is machismo or the dominant male character who was always tough, yet an artist of simple craft. I think the man is more interesting, as he tried to balance fame and humanity. His death is also a mystery which is either a 'man's choice' or a scapegoat-

escapist attitude.[26]

Thus, readers empathize with Ernest Hemingway as a man and as a legend because, for them, he is culturally relevant on some level. For some, it is the safari-hunting or drinking man who is culturally relevant; for others it is the legend that makes Hemingway an almost mythical figure.

Enduring Values and Themes

As the Hemingway legend generally expanded into his novels of the land, the sea, and the air, Hemingway himself often became the characters that thrived on values learned from what Van Wyck Brooks called a "usable past." These values could be brotherly love for the underdogs and the repressed and the victims of the wanton brutality or reliance and dependability among intimate buddies. When death came to test this bond, the hero firmly stood to uphold the preserved values to the last and battled the circumstances that life had prepared and trained him for all along. Thus, according to Mansura Mahmuda Munni, a graduate student in Linguistics in the Department of English at the University of Dhaka, Hemingway's recurring theme, "Man can be destroyed, but not defeated," corresponded to the same faith in the potential of man that is visible and espoused in the writings of Whitman, Hughes, Malamud, and Bellow. According to Munni, "This perception of man as an unyielding creation against seemingly insurmountable odds as in *The Old Man and the Sea* has elevated Hemingway to the stature of a legend in the minds of the ordinary but comprehending readers of Bangladesh and India."[27] Tawhid Shams Chowdhury, an undergraduate student in the Department of English at BRAC University, sums up how this theme of invincibility endures by means of the Hemingway legend: "Hemingway lived like a man and after his death, he became a legend."[28]

In Bangladesh and India, many faculty members and students of American literature adhere to Philip Young's thesis that the real Hemingway can be traced more snugly in his short stories than in his more celebrated novels. For example, Hemingway's stories such as "Ten Indians" and "In Another Country" depicted courage not as the "absence of fear, but as the conquering" of it; and defined hardness not as the "lack of feelings," but as the "necessary protection of a wounded mind."[29] These faculty members and students view such standards with respect and awe as something exclusive of the traditional society—standards that call for a strong, self-willed order. Hemingway's concept of style and discipline served as a guide, whether it was for writing, bullfighting, boxing, a job ethic, or simply achieving a sense of humor.

Some readers in Bangladesh and India may have accepted, albeit reluctantly, Young's thesis that Hemingway's traumatic wound caused his continual fear of death and his need to overcome it by repeatedly putting himself near danger. But this slight deviation from not so glorious a path did not distract them from their fascination with Hemingway as a man or his fictional characters because it was through this kind of defensive mechanism that these characters often withstood the "disorders of life" and thus came out as survivors. Bangladeshi and Indian readers have always admired fictional heroes that survive and move on, especially the Hemingway heroes in his most popular stories.

Critical Reactions

Since his unsettling death in 1961, Hemingway continues to be remembered in Bangladesh and India in a number of ways. First, students and teachers still discuss and debate his suicide. Second, at least one of his novels—often, *The Sun Also Rises*—is read at the Master's level in the universities. Third, many newspapers and literary journals bring out, though irregularly, supplements commemorating his death. Fourth, local writers occasionally translate his short stories and write critical articles for these newspapers and literary journals out of their own devotion to this literary giant; they cannot and do not wait for those special supplements to spur them to pay tribute.

The Hemingway legend in Bangladesh and India has been also perpetuated by the publication of a number of well-known biographies after the Nobel Laureate's death. Among these are biographies by Malcolm Cowley, Carlos Baker, A. E. Hotchner, Leicester Hemingway, and, more recently, James R. Mellow. From reading these biographies, Bangladeshi and Indian readers are particularly intrigued by the parts of his life they find bewitching: Hemingway's rebellion against his parents in Oak Park, Illinois—an older, well-established upper middle-class suburb immediately west of the city limits of Chicago; the displaying of his war wounds after his return from Italy in 1918; his four marriages; his friendships with famous personalities, such as Andre Malraux, Jean Paul Sartre, and Simone de Beauvoir; and his suicide. Learning more about the personal life of a legend has made people appreciate Hemingway as a man.

As John A. Jones and Ben R. Redman have indicated, American critics of Hemingway were negatively impressed by the public image of Hemingway that emerged in works such as *Death in the Afternoon*, *Green Hills of Africa*, and *Across the River and into the Trees*. In Bangladesh and India, the scenario was completely different. Indians, following their independence from the British rule in 1947, and Bangladeshis, following their independence from Pakistan in 1971, became mesmerized by Hemingway the man and sought additional impetus that would make him truly a legend. As Bangladesh and India became engrossed in their reconstruction, various classes of people found in Hemingway and his fictional characters a manual for living. Bangladeshis and Indians could empathize with the Hemingway heroes from Nick Adams to Jake Barnes to Santiago and beyond.

This attitude played a significant role in Bangladeshi and Indian critical reactions. Critics and the scholars were highly impressed by those novels that projected Hemingway's own viewpoints or his public image. Unlike American critics who criticized Hemingway for his lack of nonchalance and insular passion, Bangladeshi and Indian critics and scholars alike lauded him for his candidness and straight talk.

Chapter Three:
Hemingway's Short Stories in Bangladesh

Before and since the independence of Bangladesh from Pakistan in 1971, an appreciable number of Hemingway's short stories were published in Bengali translation, mostly in the literary supplements of the daily newspapers as well as in literary journals. Often, Bangladeshi editors and publishers—and to a great extent the translators—used their own discretion in choosing a particular story or in grouping the stories. Whatever the underlying reason, aesthetic considerations guided their process of selection, for without translations, works would not be accessible to readers who are not fluent in English or who do not know English at all. Some of the best-known Hemingway short stories—such as "The Short Happy Life of Francis Macomber," "The Snows of Kilimanjaro," "The Killers," "A Day's Wait," "Banal Stories," "Today is Friday," "In Another Country," "Hills Like White Elephants," "A Way You Will Never Be," and "A Clean, Well-Lighted Place"—were published separately in different dailies and literary journals in Bangladesh.

Only one anthology of Hemingway's short stories in Bengali translation supplemented these individual translations. Published by Bangla Academy in 2004, the only collection of Hemingway's stories in Bengali translation is entitled *Hemingwayr Galpa* (Stories of Hemingway). The stories—seven in all—were translated by the late Kawsar Hussain, who was an associate professor of English at Jahangirnagar University in Savar, Dhaka. Although Hussain did not state a rationale in arranging the pieces, his translations include a number of well-known stories: "The Short Happy Life of Francis Macomber," "In Another Country," "Hills Like White Elephants," "The Snows of Kilimanjaro," "A Clean, Well-Lighted Place," "Capital of the World," and "The Killers." However, in his foreword, Hussain mentioned that he had chosen the stories because Hemingway liked them in a special way. Needless to say, the collection sold well and was appreciated by scholars as well as general readers.

Threads of Life

Shahida Sultana, assistant professor of English at Jahangirnagar University School and College in Savar, Dhaka, and widow of the translator Kawsar Hussain, finds these stories to be universal because they snugly fit into the social and cultural fabric of Bangladesh. According to Sultana,

Take, for example, "The Short Happy Life of Francis Macomber." Although apparently a happy couple, each day the Macombers exchange choice words. Margaret discovers timidity and cowardliness in her husband. Margaret is aware of her strange physical beauty that has mesmerized and dwarfed Macomber. She takes advantage of this situation, becomes arbitrary and whimsical as her husband fails to rein her in. She applies complete control upon her husband. Wilson's comment is appropriate here: 'She's damn cruel, but they're all cruel. They govern, of course, and to govern one has to be cruel sometimes. Still, I've seen enough of their damn terrorism.' Although these women are in the minority, they do abound and thrive in Bangladesh. Although small in number, these women have complete dominion over their husbands. And these husbands, like Macomber, live a miserable life as they are tormented each day. Like Macomber, they only get momentary pleasure. Like Macomber, the presence of the wives terrifies their husbands and makes them nervous. They make fun of each other, call each other cowards, and call names (bitches, etc.) freely. Despite this extremity, they sustain their families—and this is possible only in countries such as Bangladesh. That all this shame, all this restlessness, and all this repentance of Macomber because of a lone mistake by him, is indeed a manifestation of sentiment to be found in Bangladesh, and perhaps in the entire Indian sub-continent. To Bangladeshi wives, the opinions of the husbands often do not have any face value. Before setting out for the safari, in response to a question by Wilson whether he wants Margot to go, Macomber remarks that it does not make any difference whether he does or not. Despite the lack of love, the house of Macomber stands out only because of the resources of Macomber and the beauty of Margaret. These two help maintain their relationship and this makes them keep going. In Bangladesh, there are many families devoid of happiness. But for some untold reason, these families survive years after years. Hemingway may come from a different country and with a different cultural baggage, but the way his characters speak in this story, their laughter and tears, their feelings of good times and bad, as well as their sense of victory and defeat, are the direct reflections of our own Bangladeshi minds.[1]

Shahida Sultana is not alone in finding a parallel between henpecked Macomber and henpecked Bangladeshi husbands. Sayma Arju, a faculty member in the English department at Stamford University in Dhaka, says that the tumultuous conjugal life of the Macombers is not unique to the American context; it goes beyond the West to other cultures of the world, including Bangladesh. According to Arju,

The likes of Macomber do exist in Bangladesh. In the social arrangement of Bangladesh, there are many married men who can be compared to Macomber. These married men, having failed in killing lions, have failed to prove their manhood. They have lost their chances. They are scared of their wives. They hate their wives, hate themselves for their predicament, and they repent constantly till they end their lives in a manner exemplified by Macomber.[2]

In "The Capital of the World," Shahida Sultana finds the youth Paco to be any young boy in Bangladesh who works in a hotel: "Hemingway has carefully developed the character of Paco and the world around him—gossip of the hotel dwellers, drinking, pimping, etc.—one clear aspect of the western society." But, according to Sultana,

> Unlike Hemingway's Paco, these Bangladeshi Pacos do not dream of becoming bullfighters, but they do dream daily nonetheless: colorful, big and small; dreams of all sorts. Half-fed and neglected as they grow up, thousands of these youths in Bangladesh earn their living in dazzling, well-lit hotels in evening work-dresses and drooling over the delicious menu beyond their reach. Like Paco, this is an incredibly realistic scenario for these young Bangladeshi hotel boys. They pass their days somehow. Suddenly their dreams are shattered as death strikes; their happiness comes to a standstill. Then they realize that they are so neglected a class that nobody would worry to rush them to the operating tables in the hospitals. Nothing slows down for them. Everybody is busy with himself as though nothing has happened.[3]

Sultana interprets this story philosophically by saying that as humans we all believe in the inevitability of death, that it may toll timely or untimely:

> As death comes at its own pace, so does life. Life moves with its own free will. All depends on the wishes of the good Lord. I believe that Hemingway's words at the end of the story would rattle the sensitivity of the Bangladeshi readers: The boy Paco had never known about any of this nor about what all these people would be doing on the next day and on other days to come. He had no idea how they really lived or how they ended. He did not even realize they ended. He died, as the Spanish phrase has it, 'full of illusions.' He had not had time in his life to lose any of them, nor even, at the end, to complete an act of contrition. This is a cruel truth. We accept this cruel truth; we all do.[4]

Like Sultana, Sayma Arju believes that the last part of the story helps readers get Hemingway's message: that is, one who does fictitious bullfights daily and erroneously thinks himself to be an expert makes a big mistake and thus brings an abrupt end to his life: "To bring about spontaneity in our dull, drab lives, we fantasize daily. But what we fantasize is indeed an unreality and this is the theme of the story."[5]

Shahida Sultana empathizes with "The Snows of Kilimanjaro:"

> I could recognize a very near and dear couple I knew as I read the story. Hemingway makes sure that Helen, from her initial liking of Harry's writings, eventually falls in love with Harry himself. Besides, having lost her first husband and son, Helen was searching for a

secure refuge in Harry. She has loved her husband one-sidedly. But even after his marriage, Harry socializes with women as before. Hurt, Helen endures it. Helen is such a woman that always goes along with her husband's likings. Having visited one of Harry's favorite spots in Africa, Helen happily says, 'Darling, you don't know how marvelous it is to see you feeling better. I couldn't stand it when you felt that way. You won't talk to me like that again, will you? Promise me?' In another place we see her cheering up and consoling her sickly husband: 'You've never lost anything. You're the most complete man I've ever known.' Harry realizes that he had mistreated her for many years. Harry's transformation, his imminent death from an incurable disease that has made him lose concentration upon anything, his reception of his wife's conversation with incredulity, Helen's patience, her deep and unyielding love for her husband, and her sense of nursing are the manifestations of a Bengali character in our country. Women in Bangladesh still adore their husbands like gods. They silently endure their husbands' ill treatment toward them. Their husbands' likes and dislikes are their own. I am fascinated to see that Hemingway has successfully spread out our typical Bengali emotions and feelings in his fiction whether he was aware of them or not. Personally, I have felt as though Helen is I, a simple, ordinary Bengali woman who has loved her husband very dearly, in her wake or sleep and has selflessly given priority to her husband's likes and dislikes. Although written in another continent, "The Snows of Kilimanjaro" has undoubtedly touched the Bengali sensibilities.[6]

In "The Snows of Kilimanjaro," Sayma Arju finds Helen to be a tragic character, a loser in her battle to keep Harry alive for her own sake:

Despite Helen's sincere efforts, she loses Harry to death. Everything appears to be meaningless to her. Helen almost loses her breath in the vortex of life and death. She waits and waits. She waits to go through the things that are going to happen. We, regardless of our race and ethnicity, wait with her too.[7]

In "In Another Country," Shahida Sultana believes that the Bangladeshi readers are familiar with the agony of the major. According to Sultana,

Having returned from the imminent attack of paralysis, the major saw his young wife die of pneumonia in a few days. When the major thinks of his loving wife, he gets lost in another world. When it comes down to marriage, he angrily says, 'A man must not marry. . . . If he is to lose everything, he should not place himself in a position to lose. He should find things he cannot lose.' Somewhere down their conversation, having failed to control himself, he pulls away his hand and goes out. But he recognizes his mistakes and asks to be forgiven. He bites his lips and says, 'It is very difficult. I cannot resign myself.' He then starts to weep. The Bangladeshi readers recognize this agony of the major. It is a common thing to reminisce about one's own dead wife. Regardless of his religion and race, everybody can feel this agony. The family bond in our country is stronger and more lasting than that of many in the west. The marital love is the basis of the couple's relationship. Nobody can accept the split that comes in death. In the family couples wander into another world where no one else can intrude. That world belongs only to the husband and wife. In this situation, we too feel like the major: deprived and dejected. We cry, cry and cry to make ourselves relieved. Consequently, each Bangladeshi reader lauds Hemingway for his universality of human feelings that cut across political boundaries.[8]

Sayma Arju believes that the characters in "In Another Country" are more psychological than physical:

Hemingway seems to have made all his characters in the stories psychoanalytical. The characters are stung with their memories and their conditions of earlier lives. In this story, the wounded soldiers knew that perhaps they would never be cured, but got treated everyday. I am unsure about their definite hopes. But I can say that the protagonist is overly confident about his own ability. He is scared of death. Although he is not a hawk, he becomes one in his fantasy and many such things. We notice that the other character in the story—that of the major—is saddened by the death of his wife. But his life does not come to a standstill; rather, it moves on. The war rages around him. And this war is for his survival and he has survived so far.[9]

A Familiar Dilemma

Bangladesh is a conservative and religious (unofficially though) country, with Islam as its dominant religion. Eighty-five percent of its population is Muslim. Like Catholicism, abortion in all its forms is strictly prohibited in Islam. But Hemingway's "Hills Like White Elephants" has made the word "abortion" a well-known phenomenon in Bangladesh, especially in today's framework. As Shahida Sultana observes,

In modern day Bangladesh, the word 'abortion,' is in our regular vocabulary, thanks to Ernest Hemingway. Often we have to resort to abortion either to save the patient's life or to neutralize the unwanted baby. Often a woman has to abort because of her physical problems. Abortion is practiced either willingly or unwillingly. Often the husband or the male figure in the family wants the abortion because he wants to spend more and longer time with his wife or his female counterpart. Often the husband feels that he will lose his wife's uninterrupted love and attention if she gives birth to a child. His wife's love and attention has to be shared with the baby. Because of the baby, his wife will not be able to give him company as before and will not be able to accompany him anywhere at the spur of the moment. For these reasons, the wife is compelled to resort to abortion. Misunderstandings arise when the wife lacks interest in doing so. Because of this issue of abortion, the two main characters of the story run into conflict between themselves. In the beginning of the story we find the two sitting face to face and looking sadly away. There is only one reason, that is, the man cannot assure the girl that the abortion is no big deal and that if she goes for it things will be all right as before. The girl says, 'And if I do it you'll be happy and things will be like they were and you'll love me?' An uncertainty permeates this girl's mind and this similar uncertainty also permeates the minds of the Bangladeshi girls. The girl in the story all along is torn by this conflict: to be or not to be. Because of the tension and nervousness, the man cannot agree with the girl about her committing the abortion. And if she does it 'it will be nice again' and the hills will look 'like white elephants.' Their agony, misunderstandings, anxiety, and restlessness have been depicted so adroitly by Hemingway that the story has conquered the souls of the Bangladeshi readers. This incident may apparently be an insignificant one for some, but it has changed our perspectives on life.[10]

Sayma Arju dances to the same tune as Shahida Sultana:

> Like Jig and her boyfriend, we have to face a similar situation. Along with the anxiety of our minds, nature also responds in a meaningful way. This feeling is quite intense. The act of abortion is not new in human culture and activity, and although we find it in this story in the American society, it is familiar as well in Bangladesh. In both cases, the pressure generally comes from the male partner and why? One lame excuse is given, that is, to continue a sound bond of love![11]

Tahsina Yasmin, a faculty member in the English department at Stamford University in Dhaka, finds "Hills like White Elephants" relevant in the context of the Bangladeshi society. According to Yasmin,

> The story is told from an objective point of view. Presented through dialogues and very little description, Hemingway shows his mastery in sketching the two characters and the psychological traits of their minds. The story presents the dilemma of a would-be mother trying to decide whether to abort the child or not—a dilemma also visible in Bangladesh nowadays.[12]

Resalath Sultana, a faculty member in the English department at Stamford University in Dhaka, finds a deeper meaning to "Hills Like White Elephants," a meaning appreciated by women in America as well as in Bangladesh. According to Resalath Sultana,

> In the story we find 'the American and the girl' converse as they wait for a train. If we dig for real meaning, we should gather that they are actually waiting for their expected good days. As the story progresses, they compare the hills with white elephants. The barren

hills that look like the white elephants is a symbol of good luck to the woman—a belief often shared also by the Bangladeshi women who are in her shoes.[13]

A Longing for Life

In "A Clean, Well-Lighted Place," Resalath Sultana finds depression to be the universal theme, a theme experienced by people in both America and Bangladesh. As Resalath explains,

> The element of depression reigns supreme in this story. A man of eighty does not want to go home at night and elects to stay at an all-night, clean, well-lighted cafe. Out of depression he tries to commit suicide, which is the reflection of Hemingway's own life. Two waiters are presented in this story. One is eager to go home and another wants to stay in the cafe. I believe this waiter wants to say that a man needs a home where he can find peace; a man needs a family where he can get love and care. At the end of the day, a man really needs such a place where he can recharge himself for the next day. Unfortunately, like many American males, many Bangladeshi males do not have such homes to go back to and are compelled to while away times in a clean, well-lighted cafe.[14]

In "A Clean, Well-Lighted," Place, Sayma Arju sees things in a little different light:

> The waiters prefer the clean, well-lighted cafe because they can appreciate the value of life. For them, earning a livelihood is more important. They are not in a hurry to go home. They love their environment so much that they can be called the termites of the cafe. On the other hand, the old man, the customer, is a different story. A week ago, the old man tried to commit suicide as he was alone and did not have a home to go back to. He has a longing for life, but at the same time he loathes it. You can find these unfortunate people everywhere even in a conservative, family-oriented country like Bangladesh.[15]

Shahida Sultana retells a personal, real-life incident that has a connection to "The Killers," emphasizing that the fear of death lurks with us on the streets everywhere. Random violence can occur at any time. Sultana relates a personal example:

> Lately, my son and I went shopping. After the shopping we went to a cafe for snacks. We were almost through eating when a group of three young men showed up at the cash register. They began to misbehave with the clerk over a trifling matter. I realized that they were the local bullies. At one point, one of them slapped the sales-clerk. Because of the deteriorating situation, we left the cafe. I did not

know what might have happened to the sales-clerk, but the day's newspapers of Bangladesh would tell you the details of the incident. Nowadays killings and assassinations are no big deal given the political atmosphere of Bangladesh. One can get killed over a minor incident. People kill and get killed freely. The killers may be apprehended, but very few are coming forward to testify in court because of retaliation. Nobody can protest this injustice for fear of his life. In "The Killers," I believe Hemingway knowingly or unknowingly has portrayed the social and political decay of Bangladesh. The rude behavior of Max and Al toward the employees—Nick, George, and Sam—of the hotel takes me back to Bangladesh. During their conversation Nick learns that Max and Al are here to kill Ole Anderson, although they do not know the identity of their forthcoming victim. Ironically, they are out to get, an act as heinous as can be, Ole Anderson only because he has betrayed a friend. The same things are happening in Bangladesh. When the killers fail to locate Ole Anderson, they leave and Nick readies to deliver this situation-report to him, the cook anxiously says, 'You better not have anything to do with it at all, Sam. You better stay way out of it.' We say the same thing in Bangladesh. Thus Hemingway is a writer for all countries of the world. His subject matter, presentation, character delineation, characters' passion, emotions and feelings, happiness and remorse, and fear—all of these have made him universal. His writings have not been confined to a specific geographic boundary; rather, they have conquered the heart and soul of each sensitive reader where he is and lives.[16]

Sayma Arju finds the fear of death in "The Killers" as a common phenomenon in all men and in all ages. According to Arju,

> The fear of death has been the same among us and will be so no matter where we are, although we are helpless against it. The pathological part of it is that the killers—Max and Al—want to know about their victim before they will finish him off. This is not to say that the interest in this type of fancy killing is rare. This type of incident is normal in any society and in any social context, Bangladesh included.[17]

In "The Killers," Resalath Sultana finds "an exceptional philosophy of life" in the face of death. As Sultana explains, "Ole Anderson is not a coward; he is tough, for he is willing to go outside to die."[18] Men should not be afraid of death. When death comes they should face it courageously.

The Appeal of Translations

Because of its non-British, non-colonial origin, the American short story did not at first fare well in the syllabi of the English departments at the colleges and universities in Bangladesh. Consequently, the reaction of Bangladeshi scholars and educated readers to the first translation of Hemingway short stories soon after 1971 was very limited and often insignificant. But Hemingway's short fiction has appeared in translation from time to time in the newspapers and magazines in Bangladesh. Since the independence of Bangladesh in 1971, Kawsar Hussain's translation of *Hemingwayr Galpa* (Stories of Hemingway) is the only single-volume translation of Hemingway's stories.

In reviewing Kawsar Hussain's translation of *Hemingwayr Galapa* (Stories of Hemingway), all of the four critics and faculty—Shahida Sultana, Sayma Arju, Resalath Sultana, and Tahsina Yasmin—pointed out the huge popularity of the stories selected, lauded Hemingway's skill and dexterity in making the details of a situation or event amazingly real, and added that these are some of the traits that show that Hemingway was a writer of the highest caliber. These four critics detect a superhuman personality of Hemingway in these translations and label them as some the most realistic of the stories. But they agree on one thing: that is, the translation of "The Killers" lost its symmetry and beauty because of the lack of slang equivalents in Bengali.[19]

The fact remains that the Hussain translation brought about a dramatic change in the Bangladeshi critical approach to the short story art of Ernest Hemingway. As Shahida Sultana states,

> The contributions of Hemingway to the short story are as important as those of Edgar Allan Poe. The Bangladeshi readers, whether they are college English majors or just casual readers, recognize Hemingway because he introduced a brand new, concrete prose, with simple, assertive sentences to the short story, and making his characters introspective and by making them less and less reliant on the role of the plot. If we take the example of "Hills Like White Elephants," we find that the understanding of the story rests upon the epiphany as well as upon the atmosphere, not upon the traditional unraveling of a story through a series of plots, which is a landmark of the British short story.[20]

Sultana's insights into the short stories by Hemingway echo the assertion by Frank O' Connor that Hemingway's stories indeed lack "a subject."[21] Another story that can be mentioned to highlight the methodology employed by Hemingway is "The Killers." Instead of telling the theme too easily, Hemingway builds suspense, uses skillful dialogue and relevant details. In addition, he keeps his emotions detached to let the readers participate. These are the cardinal reasons why the majority of the faculty members, students, and general readers in Bangladesh believe that Hemingway is one of the inventors of the modern short story form. And this is one good reason why his stories should be studied at the high school, college, and university levels in Bangladesh. The opinion of the faculty, students, and readers prevailed as we see at least one or two of Hemingway stories are taught at the undergraduate and graduate levels.

Previously, Bangladeshis had known little about Hemingway's early life to tie him in with his fictional characters. But with the publication of some of the early Nick Adams stories and the monumental *The Old Man and the Sea* in

1952, Bangladeshis changed their minds about Hemingway. With a new zeal, they began to take a new look at him and his writing. By the time he received the Nobel Prize for Literature in 1954, following the publication of *The Old Man and the Sea*, his short stories had taken a strong foothold in Bengali universities and critical circles, and Hemingway was at the top of his popularity. As a result, Bengalis were much more responsive and appreciative.

It is generally agreed that the number of Hemingway academic critics and general scholars in Bangladesh are in short supply; but almost all of them concur that the autobiographical elements are strewn across Hemingway's fiction. Zerin Alam, associate professor of English at the University of Dhaka and a Hemingway scholar points out for her fellow Bengalis that "Up in Michigan" was Hemingway's first published piece that contained psychological conflicts.[22] These psychological conflicts later became typical of his subsequent writing. Alam does well in pinpointing the autobiographical elements in the Nick Adams stories in "In Our Time" and in *The Fifth Column and the First Forty-nine Stories*, and in interpreting the inherent meaning of the ritual Nick follows in "Big Two-Hearted River," but she does not offer a detailed analysis of Hemingway's writing technique. She, however, simply states that the writing technique has made Hemingway's short stories unique in the world, especially for the readership in Bangladesh.

Tahmina Ahmed, associate professor of English at the University of Dhaka and a Hemingway critic, like other Bangladeshi readers, attaches importance to what is apparently insignificant and to the qualities that separate Hemingway from early American realists and many of his subsequently failed imitators. In "The Killers," Ahmed detects Hemingway's effective use of hard details; that is, the gangsters' gloves, which they leave behind, or the swelled sawed-off shotgun under Al's coat. Ahmed goes on to say that another technique Hemingway employs is an allusion to a subject, leaving the details for the reader to figure out.[23]

This is evident in the way Hemingway depicts the character of Ole Anderson, who hovers between despair and hopelessness. We only have a visual impression in Ole Anderson's eyes and in his single swing toward the wall; but with this swing, Ole displays his submission to imminent death. By blending style and technique so skillfully with the contents of the story, Hemingway, Ahmed maintains, probably has achieved the possible fourth or fifth dimension that he believes an author is capable of.[24] This illustrates the fact that Hemingway's stories have become a part of the experience of the person who reads them.

One of the few writers in Bangladesh that Hemingway has directly influenced is Syed Shamsul Haque. One the foremost novelists and short story writers of Bangladesh, Haque admires Hemingway so much that in his short story entitled *Firay Ashay* (One Who Returns) he names the narrator "Hemingway." In the following excerpt from *Firay Ashay*, "Hemingway" is juxtaposed in the plot and behaves like a Bangladeshi (indeed, he is a native Bengali):

'After a long time Abdullah said, "Hemingway?"'

'What?'

'Forget it.'

'I have.'

'No, you haven't.'

'Yes, I have.'

'All right, then laugh. You are a writer. You want to be a great writer! You must learn how to laugh. Why don't you laugh, Hemingway?'[25]

Although Haque does not juxtapose 'Hemingway' as a character in any other story, the excerpt above shows the length and breadth of the influence of Hemingway as a man in the world of fiction in Bangladesh. Note the short sentences and the lack of "he said, she said." This is pure Hemingway.

Besides Haque, Humayun Ahmed, perhaps the most popular fiction writer of Bangladesh, is also affected by the Hemingway magic. In one of his television plays, Ahmed very much fashions his character Yunus of Nandail (Jonah of Nandail, although the biblical and Koranic name, Jonah, does not carry any religious implications in the television-play) after either Max or Al in Hemingway's "The Killers." There are parallels between the Hemingway story and the Ahmed television-play. There are two hired guns in "The Killers" as against one in Ahmed's play. In "The Killers," we know a great deal of symbolic meaning through the movement of Ole Anderson, the intended victim of Max and Al. This story is unique because Hemingway employs a method that allows the gestures of his characters to speak for their feelings. Indeed, we know more about Ole Anderson's past and present through Nick's conversations with his associates in the restaurant, including Mrs. Bell, the caretaker of Ole Anderson's house. Max and Al are two ruthless, deliberate killers who just want to kill their victim and be through with it.

In the Ahmed play, *Yunus of Nandail*, the lone hired gun, is rather open-minded and humane, as he wants to find out more about his victim before he finishes him off. As the play progresses, we come to know more about the imminent victim through Yunus's straightforward questioning and conversing with him. In doing so, Ahmed, unlike Hemingway, infuses a little bit of comic relief in his play. It is quite ironic that the killers—Max and Al and Yunus of Nandail—in both cases have never met their victims before and thus are strangers to them. Because the victims do not personally know their killers, perhaps this should minimize the agony of their deaths. Both Hemingway and Ahmed appear to be saying that the killers, no matter what color and whether American or Bangladeshi, may be either brutal or a little humane in their execution of death, but they are killers nonetheless. Death is always tough no matter how it occurs.

In an attempt to through new light on Hemingway's short stories, some Bangladeshi-critics such as Kaiser Haque and Shahida Sultana label Hemingway as an existentialist.[26] The preponderance of subjectivity in rationalizing all truth, the disappearance of objectivity, and existential fear are all trademarks of the Hemingway hero, according to Kaiser Haque, who goes on to say that Hemingway's existentialism emanates from his own war experience and also reflects the main trends and tendencies of his time. Ironically, Hemingway's own war experience and the psyche of his era found its philosophical expression in existentialism. Contrast and parallelism, according to Haque, give Hemingway ample means to advance his own brand of existentialism: contrast gives him the leeway to pit the hero against traditionalism, conventions, artificialities, and lies, while paralleling characters allows him to take nihilistic experiences from individual, subjective experience and make them conditions of all rational men.[27]

One of the most recent distinctive critical approaches to Hemingway was the emphasis placed by the critics on the existential framework, the complex structural principles, and the naturalistic symbols that they traced in individual stories. These critics, including general readers, believe that Hemingway's stories overwhelmingly achieved a perfect balance between form and content. They demonstrated this in their criticism and polemics of literature, and thus made important contributions to an understanding of his art. According to Haque and Shahida Sultana, Hemingway was one of the architects in the development of the modern American short story. By using short terse dialogue, avoiding dense concentrated narrative, and scooping miscellaneous undertones, he elevated the naturalistic-concrete to the symbolic level, and so transformed the early, fledgling short story into an art form that crossed the geographical and cultural boundaries as far as Bangladesh.[28]

Thus, the re-introduction of Hemingway's short stories in translation has given rise to a critical recognition of Hemingway's work as both modern and contemporary in its style, subject matter, and human appeal. Bangladeshi men and women alike can empathize with his stories; and as Bangladeshi society changes, they see their reflections in the characters and depictions of war and society. In their appeal to the Bangladeshi psyche, Hemingway's stories transcend geographical, racial and ethnic boundaries. One might go so far to say that Hemingway could even be a homeboy, someone to whom Bangladeshi readers can easily relate, unlike William Faulkner, whose *Sound and Fury* would be impenetrable—alien, "Greek," regional, and culturally myopic.

Chapter Four:
Hemingway's Short Stories in India

Hemingway's short stories not only have won the hearts and minds of critics, general readers, and scholars in Bangladesh, but also the admiration, appreciation and respect of critics, general readers, and scholars in India. Since the days of pre-independence—before 1947—and post-independence—after 1947—critics, general readers, and scholars in India have always liked Hemingway's short stories. Unlike Bangladesh, where mass literacy is comparatively much lower than in India, Indian readers are familiar with Hemingway's writings without translations. This is indeed an advantage for Indian readers over Bangladeshi readers who, to comprehend Hemingway, rely on English versions as well as translations.

As Hemingway the man slowly but steadily grew into a legend, Indian readers and academic critics became fascinated by his short stories. As the short story became a national art form in American literature in the late 19th century, its impact was felt as far away as India. Hemingway was one of the major catalysts in making Indian readers appreciative of the modern American short story, especially the unique and inimitable Hemingway variety. In "Big Two-Hearted River," for example, as Philip Young rightly observes and Indian readers concur, the style "is the perfect expression of the content of the story:" When Nick is camping or eating his breakfast with deliberate care and concentration on each detail, the sentences are short and the rhythm is monotonous. When he loses a trout and is excited, the sentences become shorter and tense. Later, when he succeeds in catching a good trout and the pressure is off, making him relaxed, the sentences lengthen and become appropriately graceful.[1]

Another stylistic trait of Hemingway that Indian readers and academic critics noticed and liked was Hemingway's art of writing simple sentences and avoiding ornamentation. Hemingway started writing with "the truest sentence" that he could think of and thought, "If I started to write elaborately, or like someone introducing or presenting something, I found that I could cut that scroll-work or ornament out and throw it away and start with the first true simple declarative sentence I had written."[2] As critic Syed Ali Hamid states, "The lack of ornamentation is more than compensated for by a clever use of irony and understatement, which makes his stories highly suggestive, and gives to them something of the intensity of the lyric."[3] Hemingway believed that if you hold back some information from the reader, it strengthens the story: "You could omit anything if you knew what you omitted, and the omitted part would strengthen the story and make people feel something more than they understood."[4] As Carlos Baker remarks, "He learned how to get the most from the least, how to prune language and avoid waste motion, how to multiply intensities, and how to tell nothing but the truth in a way that always allowed for telling more than the truth."[5]

Indian readers recognize that in many of his stories, for example, "Hills Like White Elephants," Hemingway aims at maximal objectivity. As Hamid observes,

> The story progresses mainly through dialogue and the writer, focusing dispassionately on a particular point in the life of the characters, does not intrude with his comments. Sherwood Anderson had already rebelled against the magazine formula plot story and had ushered in the modern short story in America. Ernest Hemingway, by his superb craftsmanship developed and established the modern short story.[6]

In the minds of Indian readers, Hemingway is one of the truest and most original practitioners of the short story form.

Thematic Concerns

Descriptively, the Indian academic critic Hamid has divided Hemingway's short stories into six phases or periods. The first phase started with the publication of the six untitled miniatures in the *Little Review Exiles' Number* in April 1923, and ended with the publication of "In Our Time" in October 1925. In a number of the stories in this volume, the protagonist is a young boy named Nick Adams. Some stories depict Nick's boyhood experiences at home in the American Midwest. Others deal with war and alienation in which Nick is "war-torn, disillusioned and in a state of spiritual bankruptcy." According to Hamid, during this first phase,

> It seems that Hemingway had included the stories of his protagonist's adolescence and early youth to provide a more comprehensive focus, a fullness, to his protagonist. The Nick Adams stories, for example, are related to each other and may be said to depict the progressive development of the Hemingway hero. In short, the stories and miniatures of this phase reflect Hemingway's major thematic concerns.[7]

The second phase of his short fiction falls between 1926 and 1927, when Hemingway wrote fourteen short stories published under the title *Men without Women* (1927). This collection contained two longer stories, "Fifty Grand" and "The Undefeated." Hamid notes, "The stories of this phase predominantly deal with Hemingway's ethos."[8] These include stories such as "The Undefeated," "Fifty Grand," "In Another Country" and "The Killers." In the first two, the protagonists are aging professionals: a bullfighter and a boxer, respectively. During this phase, Hamid observes, "In all these stories, Hemingway puts his protagonists in situations when they have to rely completely on their own inner resources and in this way brings out their inner character."[9]

The third phase of Hemingway's short fiction covers the period between 1932 and 1933, during which he wrote fourteen stories published under the title *Winner Take Nothing* (1933). A mood of despair and alienation permeates these stories, especially "A Clean, Well-Lighted Place" and "The Gambler, the Nun and the Radio." Between 1927 and 1932, Hemingway seems to have lost his positive view of dying with honor and assumed one of despair.

The fourth phase of Hemingway's short fiction began and ended in 1936, when he published three longer stories, "The Capital of the World," "The Snows of Kilimanjaro," and "The Short Happy Life of Francis Macomber." The latter two are stories of redemption, and Hemingway's stories of this phase highlight cherished human values. In "The Snows of Kilimanjaro," Harry, who had wasted his talent as a writer by giving himself up to an easy life, struggles to redeem himself moments before his death. In "The Short Happy Life of Francis Macomber," the protagonist, Francis Macomber, who has lived a life of cowardice under the domination of women, redeems himself by conquering his fear and cowardice hunting buffalo in Africa. Reflecting on this phase, Hamid states, "Perhaps in these short stories, Hemingway brings out his concept of man and the values that should inspire him."[10]

The fifth phase of Hemingway's short fiction coincides with his assignment in Spain between 1937 and 1938 to cover the Spanish Civil War (1936) as a journalist. The stories from this period are set in Spain during the Civil War and their dominant theme is war. One of the stories, "Old Man at the Bridge" was included in the collection *The Fifth Column and the First Forty-Nine Stories* (1938). Four more were collected posthumously in *The Fifth Column and Four Stories of the Spanish Civil War* (1969).

For a decade following the publication of *For Whom the Bell Tolls* (1940), Hemingway did not publish any short fiction. It is surmised that he had dried up his sources of inspiration. Yet the sixth and last phase of his short fiction writing yielded his masterpiece, *The Old Man and the Sea*, which was published in 1952 in the September issue of the *Life* magazine and brought out as a book the same year. As Hamid observes, "Through the struggle of the old fisherman with the giant marlin and the sharks, Hemingway showed his high regard for the values of courage and sacrifice in the midst of trial. Santiago emerges as a man of heroic stature, the essence of the Hemingway hero."[11] After writing *The Old Man and the Sea*, Hemingway did not publish any significant work.

In addition to these six phases of writing, Syed Ali Hamid classifies Hemingway's short fiction thematically according to four categories: alienation, love, resignation, and affirmation. Hamid explains the rationale of his study of Hemingway's short fiction as follows:

> A study of the themes in his short fiction is important because
> Hemingway deals with the same themes both in his short fiction and

his novels. It is important to note that Hemingway started his literary career as a short story writer and his earliest short stories reflect his principal thematic concerns. In a broad sense his fiction embodies his quest of the hero and the hero of the short fiction is further developed in his novels as the novel provides a larger context in which the characters can be placed and developed. This romantic quest of the hero was for Hemingway an inverted form of a search for identity.[12]

The Crucible of War

As Hemingway himself explained, the reason he wrote so extensively about war was because it constituted the main activity of his time. Indeed, Hemingway had witnessed war throughout much of his lifetime. Although he was frequently exposed to war from an early age, he always hated it. According to Hamid, "It is this hatred for war that forms an important aspect of his fiction, and the war had such a pronounced effect on his mind that even when it is not being dealt with directly, its shadow is always lurking in the background."[13] Taking into account only his short fiction, several stories in his volume of complete stories, eight out of the sixteen vignettes of *In Our Time*, and his posthumously published volume of Spanish Civil War stories, *The Fifth Column* and *The First Forty-Nine Stories*, deal with war.

As Hamid explains, "The war in the epic sense appealed to Hemingway as an opportunity to bring out the best in man. But the experience of war soured him considerably. Hemingway worshipped courage and the spectacle of bloodshed caused through machines was no war, it was mass murder."[14] In the following vignette, Hemingway describes how wars were fought in his day:

> We were in a garden at Mons. Young Buckley came in with his patrol from across the river. The first German I saw climbed up over the garden wall. We waited till he got one leg over and then potted him. He had so much equipment on and looked awfully surprised and fell down into the garden. Then three more came over further down the wall. We shot them. They all came just like that.[15]

This passage shows Hemingway's disgust for modern warfare as a cruel inhuman game that amount to nothing but cold-blooded murder. Where is honor in death when it occurs like this? What must be the effects on men who fight in wars?

In another passage, Hemingway describes a situation in which a barricade is jammed across a bridge: "A big wrought-iron grating from the front of a house. Too heavy to lift and you could shoot through it and they would have to climb over it. It was absolutely topping. They tried to get over it, and we potted them from forty yards."[16] It is all right to shoot from a distance of forty yards when the enemies are not even in a position to shoot back. The inhumanity overpowers the senses.

In several stories, Hemingway also provides us glimpses of the carnage on the battlefield. In "A Natural History of the Dead," for example, Hemingway puts on the tone of a naturalist studying the dead. As Hamid describes it,

> The narrative is again controlled, detached and brutal, with an underlying irony. He gives us an idea of the insensibility of much fighting that took place in the First World War by describing the Austrian offensive of June 1918 in Italy in which first a withdrawal was forced and later an advance made so that the positions before and after the battle were exactly the same. The only difference was that a large number of people died. This makes it not only horrifying but also an exercise in futility. He describes scenes of horror unique to war.[17]

Although they are eventually buried, the dead lay strewn on the field and change color:

> The color change in Caucasian races is from white to yellow, to yellow-green to black. If left long enough in the heat the flesh comes to resemble coal-tar, especially where it has been broken or torn, and it has quite a visible tar-like iridescence. The dead grow larger each day until sometimes they become quite too big for their uniforms, filling these until they seem blown tight enough to burst. . . . The surprising thing next to their progressive corpulence is the amount of paper that is scattered about the dead. . . . The heat, the flies, the indicative positions of the bodies in the grass, and the amount of paper scattered are impressions one retains.[18]

Hemingway's detached tone of narration adds to the horror of the scene. He comes to the conclusion that in modern mechanized warfare, "most men die like animals, not men."[19] According to Hamid, this leads to despair:

> Hemingway expresses the loss of faith in God when one comes across such scenes of horror on the battlefield. In an ironic tone, he cites the example of Mungo Park, the persevering traveler, who had written how he was inspired by the beauty and the very presence of a mass plant in the desert, it gave him a renewed faith in life and God at a time when he was about to give up due to hunger and fatigue. Mungo Park had asked this question to himself and it gave him confidence.[20]

Thus, in "A Natural History of the Dead," the narrator pleads, "Can that being who planted, watered and brought to perfection, in this obscure part of the world, a thing which appears of so small importance, look with unconcern upon the situation and suffering of creatures formed after His own image? Surely not."[21] Later the narrator cynically asks, "One wonders what that persevering traveler, Mungo Park, would have seen on a battlefield in hot weather to restore his confidence."[22]

In such passages, Hamid observes Hemingway's existential predicament: "Here Hemingway is hinting at that widespread feeling of apathy towards established religion which could not give the answers to such questions, and the rejection of which is echoed in the declaration of the death of God by Nietzsche."[23] The critic N. Ramchandran Nair finds that in "A Natural History of the Dead," "Hemingway implicitly advances the thesis that a keen awareness of death obliges one to lead a more rigorous life."[24] His characters, however, in rigorous activity become almost frantic.

In "The Butterfly and the Tank," Hemingway again shows us the impact of war on human beings. According to Hamid, this story, set in Madrid during the Spanish Civil War, depicts how "during the war, people live under such abnormal conditions that it would be a mistake to expect them to behave normally. The constant fear of death and exposure to horror makes them behave in a heartless manner."[25] At the end of the story, the narrator reflects upon Pedro's wife as she cries and asks, "Pedro, Pedro. Who has done this to thee?" We can only speculate that the police would not be able to tell her, even if they knew the name of the man who shot him. According to Hamid, "The narrator clearly implies that it is not the individual but the war that is responsible for this utter chaos."[26]

In other stories, Hemingway projects the state of mind of men who have fought in the war. Nick Adams in "A Way You'll Never Be," for example, has fought in the war and has also been wounded. As Hamid observes,

> He has seen unimaginable scenes of horror and bloodshed in the war and this traumatic experience of being wounded has affected his mind. He is in a critical mental condition. He gets fits of insanity and he desperately tries to hold them off. . . . Nick's subsequent wounding was the final blow to his already battered mind. It makes him lose his mental balance.[27]

In the thought-passages, that is, the confused workings of Nick's mind wherever he lies down to take rest, there is a recurrent image of a yellow house, a stable and a river, one that frightens him:

> What frightened him so that he could not get rid of it were that long yellow house and the different width of the river. Now he was back here at the river, he had gone through that same town, and there was no house. Nor was the river that way. Then where did he go each night and what was the peril, and why should he wake, soaking wet, more frightened than he had ever been in a bombardment, because of a house and a long stable and a canal?[28]

The answer is provided in his last thought-passage in the story, where the image of a yellow house, a stable and a river is associated with his wounding:

> He shut his eyes and in the place of the man with the beard who looked at him over the sights of the rifles, quite calmly before

squeezing off, the white flash and clublike impact, on his knees, hot-sweet choking, coughing it on to the rock while they went past him, he saw a long, yellow house with a low stable and the river much wider than it was and stiller.[29]

Nick apparently associates death with tranquil paradise; the only place that he knows is safe, home. Because the images are associated with his wounding and the fear of death, they frighten him. Hamid observes, "This wounding will have a life-long impact on the mind of the Hemingway protagonist, as it had on Hemingway himself, who was also wounded in the First World War, and would change the course of his life altogether"[30] Nair agrees, "The wound obviously is a manifestation of his [Nick's] intense, incessant suffering and struggle."[31]

Another classic symbolic statement of the fear that lies at the heart of so much that Hemingway has written is vividly seen through Nick in "Now I Lay Me." Nick is no longer the man he was; he is a miniature self now. He now cannot sleep without a light because his mind is paralyzed with the fear of death, of feeling that "if I ever shut my eyes in the dark and let myself go, my soul would go out of my body. I had been that way for a long time, ever since I had been blown up at night and felt it go out of me and go off and then come back."[32] As Nair observes, "The Hemingway hero with a physical or psychic wound is a loner in the dark."[33]

The wound, then, may be a symbol of the hardships and suffering of life, a theme with universal appeal, with which Indians can immediately identify. India has also known the chaos of war because it fought a series of wars with its neighbors, Pakistan and China. Having known the horrors of war, and having dealt with them for generations, it seems almost instinctual that the shadows of war cast upon Hemingway's stories would lead his Indian readers to reflect upon these stories in terms of their own experience fighting the two major wars against their next-door neighbors in 1965 and 1971.

In war, besides the soldiers, the civilians also go through tremendous sufferings. In several stories and vignettes, Hemingway has portrayed the destruction precipitated by war, resulting in the displacement of the civilian population. In "On the Quai at Smyrna," for instance, Hemingway describes the evacuation of refugees from Smyrna in the war between Greece and Turkey in 1922. Hamid notes that "Hemingway depicts scenes of horror, the brutalities and the immense sufferings that human beings have to endure during war."[34] Nair notes that in the Smyrna piece there are the "numbness, the horror and the thoughtless drift of humans trapped in war-situations. They affirm the extremely painful when not the stupefying conditions of contemporary man's life causing impasse, decay and death."[35] For example, there is an episode at the end of the story where a woman is giving birth to a child and a young girl is holding a blanket over her and crying. This may be a small episode, but it serves to magnify and symbolize the sufferings of the people during an evacuation. And, we might note, the girl is crying over a birth.

Modern warfare causes widespread destruction of men and material, leading to the uprooting of the civilian population. Civilians become helpless victims, suffering through no fault of their own, like the seventy-six year old man in "Old Man at the Bridge," another story of the Spanish Civil War. He has been forced to leave his hometown because of the war. He has to suffer, though he is "without politics" and has nothing to do with the war. As Hamid says, "The old man here becomes a symbol of the suffering and helplessness of human beings because of war."[36] Anyone who has lived through a war fought around his home will immediately recognize these feelings.

The last paragraph makes the inevitability of suffering all the more emphatic, for the reference to Easter Sunday gives the story Christian connotations and strong irony. As Hamid observes,

> Easter Sunday, in Christianity, is a symbol of the resurrection of Christ to help and lead people. But in the story, the irony is that the old man is utterly helpless. The narrator reflects that the only luck he has is that he need not worry about his cats as they can take care of themselves and it being overcast, the enemy planes will not be in operation in time for bombardment. But this is only temporary because the Fascist troops are advancing towards the bridge and reach there. Hemingway's use of irony heightens the pathos of the situation, making the old man the victim of savage forces unleashed by war.[37]

He speaks here not only for Christians, but all who suffer the existential brunt of senseless killing.

Another story where Hemingway has portrayed the state of mind of men who have fought in the war and have realized that modern warfare is so utterly insensible that taking part in it amounts to nothing more than suicide is "Under the Ridge:"

> We had been with those who lay there waiting for the tanks that did not come; waiting under the inrushing shriek and roaring crash of the shelling; the metal and the earth thrown like clods from a dirt fountain; and overhead the cracking, whispering fire like curtain. We know how those felt, waiting. They were as forward as they could get. And man could not move further and live, when the order came to move ahead.[38]

Finally, in the short stories dealing with war, Hemingway focuses attention on both aspects of war—what it does to the non-combatants and the effects on the soldiers themselves. For the non-combatants or the civilian population, war brings untold miseries to all regardless of their age or gender, killing them and displacing them, burning their abodes, which in turn causes destruction and ruination of the landscape. As for the combatants, it exposes them to wanton brutalities, which leads to callousness, resulting in psychic disintegration. Hamid summarizes Hemingway's depictions of the psychic numbing brought on by war:

It would be important to note that in the war stories, the protagonist is usually a soldier, probably an extension of Hemingway himself seeking an opportunity for personal heroism and dignity through sacrifice. The short stories reveal with brutal force the death of this ideal. In surveying the plight both of the combatant and non-combatant in modern war, Hemingway projects the picture of that utter disaster which brought humanity to ruin and laid the foundations for a period of unmitigated spiritual decay which became the symptom of our age. This is done as much by the pervasive wisdom of his vision as by sticking to an austere style, which has been shorn of all emotional excess and in the repetitive rhythm of which echo the footfalls of the lamentable history of war that affects the inner and the outer world of man. Hemingway's stance as a short story writer is to create through muted irony and a scrupulous adherence to the laws of realism that sense of despair and despondency in which all that is genuine and true in human nature is laid waste and the animal in man surfaces, ready to devour all that is good and noble in human nature. The war stories of Hemingway in the intensity of their focus bring out the insane brutality of war in a style that eschews emotion, symbol, or rhetorical suggestiveness so that an ominous impression of fright and horror, of waste and chaos emerges, resembling the dazed vacuous gaze of Nick Adams for whom the overwhelming sense of loss is too deep for tears or shallow rhetoric.[39]

Hamid goes on to say that Hemingway mastered the power of the unspoken word:

It is in his short stories that Hemingway gradually learned something of the power of the unspoken word that illumines and brings home with greater force the vast meanings of the dog-weary syllables that stumble and gasp, gasp and stumble like the old man in "Old Man at the Bridge" and whose sheer exhaustion tells a story of suffering that the artist in Hemingway wisely refrains from attempting to narrate. The sheer magnitude of suffering that the war stories of Hemingway encompass with such abundant economy and precision makes reading of them something of a lyric experience.[40]

And having gone through three major wars with China and Pakistan, both the civilian population and the soldiers of India who fought them know first-hand what war is all about and that war is definitely not "a lyric experience" but an indelible reality.

Alienation is an important element in Hemingway's fiction. Alienation explains the peculiar behavior of some of the central figures of his short stories; it also indicates the moral and spiritual vacuum brought about by the First World War to an entire generation known as the "lost generation." As Hamid observes,

The war brought about a total disintegration and loss of faith in the established values resulting in a spiritual vacuum. After witnessing the terrible scenes on the battlefield man could no longer believe in

God's mercy and His infinite goodness. The Hemingway protagonist
feels that the only sensible thing would be to dissociate himself from
this stupid and insane war before he goes completely out of his mind,
and we come across Nick badly wounded and disillusioned, declaring
his separate peace. It is this separate peace, which represents a state
of alienation.[41]

Like Indian soldiers who fought three major wars against neighboring China and
Pakistan, the central figure in a Hemingway story often returns from the
battlefield a metamorphosed man. Krebs, for example, in "Soldier's Home,"
returns to his hometown in Oklahoma after participating in the war and
discovers that "the world they were in was not the world he was in."[42] Ironically,
the place he has returned to is no longer a 'home' to him. He is a complete
stranger in his own hometown, even to his parents, who cannot understand him
any longer. When he recounts his war stories to them, they are nonchalant about
them. Even the townspeople are fed up with so many exaggerated war stories
that they show little interest in Krebs's experiences no matter how true they may
be. The situation that saved him in war has wounded him at home. Many of us
have experienced the same quandary.

Hemingway's preoccupation with alienation and the alienated individual,
the *nada* or "the state of nothingness in which man finds himself in a world
devoid of any order, and his concern with the problem of finding values by the
individual himself has led to his affinities with existentialism, an important and
influential philosophical movement of the twentieth century."[43] Hemingway's
"A Clean, Well-Lighted Place" is an example in the existentialist mode.
According to Hamid, "It is a dramatic exposition of the chaos and disorder
prevailing in the world, loss of faith in the established values, and the state of
nothingness that man finds himself in."[44] The story moves on through dialogue
between two waiters in a cafe, one older and one younger, about an old man,
who, being alone lately, does not have a place to go back to and sits drinking till
late each night. We have no evidence of this, only that he has not a wife. Hamid
adds that

> the clean, well-lighted café here becomes a symbol of order and
> refuge, a tiny spot in the middle of the huge, overbearing darkness
> outside. The surrounding darkness becomes a symbol of the chaos
> resulting from the widespread disintegration of values. The spiritual
> void or the nothingness is a consequence of the collapse of the
> prevailing system. . . . The story is a sad commentary on the post-war
> man who finds himself so utterly helpless that he finds it difficult
> even to hold himself together.[45]

Like the old man in the café, modern-day Indian men who are wifeless and lack
a home to return to belong to the "club" headed by the old man and the older
waiter in the story above.

Although the old man and the older waiter in "A Clean, Well-Lighted
Place," need a clean, well-lighted café for the night, Frazer in "The Gambler, the

Nun, and the Radio" plays the radio every night. According to Hamid, "He is also one of those who have realized the lack of relevance of any prevailing pattern that sustains society and, therefore, find it in complete disarray."[46] This is discernable from Frazer's observations in the last part of the story. As Hamid explains,

> These observations, having Marxian echoes, point towards that total rejection of society along with all the things that go with it, which was the most significant feature of the postwar man. But while Marx could point towards a viable alternative to mankind, Mr. Frazer is unable to do so. What matters to him, at this stage, is to keep himself under control. In order to achieve this, he searches for occupations that would keep him engaged so that he would succeed in preventing himself from thinking. His wish to preserve the same two views from the window of his room in the hospital shows the extent of his yearning for some sense of order.[47]

Some of Hemingway's stories show his protagonist striving to recover and rejuvenate himself. In "Big Two-Hearted River," for instance, Nick is alone in a specter world where a shadow of his former self roams, trying to find his bearings, after his terrifying experiences in the war. As Hamid observes, "In a society whose very framework has collapsed, it is not possible to redeem oneself by any collective action. It is the lone individual who can seek his own salvation, by his refusal to accept defeat, by reasserting his individuality through desperate acts of courage and reaffirming his faith in himself."[48]

Nick has made at least an impressive beginning. In Hemingway, alienation is not a state of unredeemable condition; through fresh trials of strength and endurance, man can get over it and start anew. Yes, for Nick, the nightmare is real; so also is the hope that "tomorrow is another day."[49] Such a positive affirmation is what Indians have come to accept.

Love and Its Conflicts

Next come Hemingway's love stories. It is generally recognized by common readers, Indians included, that Hemingway's short fiction reflects male-dominated relationships where women play a sidelined minor role. Hamid describes this genre of his output as "largely hero-oriented, and the protagonists conform to the aggressively male stereotype so dear to Hemingway."[50] A good amount of his short fiction is sugarcoated with love. What comes out of these love stories, however, is that the protagonists fail in their love-relationship. Spurred by the notion of love, Hemingway's heroes are initially tempted by the idea of being in love. This is the case in a hero-oriented male-dominated world like that of Hemingway, as well as of India. As Hamid observes,

> A love relationship involves a certain amount of give and take,

sacrifice and responsibility. But the Hemingway protagonist is so constituted that he shirks away from attachments. . . . This leads to a failure in the love relationship as the Hemingway protagonist takes a step towards forming a love relationship without wanting to bear any responsibility. He wants to take without giving. He does not want the woman to demand anything from him, but expects her to be subservient, undemanding and to leave him free. But a proper love relationship is a two-way affair. Thus when the relationship leads to attachment and obligations it arouses a conflict in the Hemingway protagonist and leads to the break-up or failure of the relationship. This failure indicates the failure of character as distinguished from the failure of situation in which circumstances outside the control of two loving hearts intervene tragically to bring their relationship to an end as in Romeo and Juliet.[51]

Hemingway's "The End of Something," for instance, shows Nick breaking up his love relationship with Marjorie, and withdrawing from a relationship after he had taken a step toward building it. After all, Nick reserves the right to the eventual freedom from any kind of obligation. According to Hamid,

To claim supreme freedom for his male protagonists to involve or de-involve (sic) themselves at will in a deeply personal relationship like love shows Hemingway either did not accept the sanctity and depth of love-relationship or he saw clearly that as characters his protagonists do not have it in them to enter into normal human relationships like normal human beings. . . . In love-relationships Hemingway protagonists reveal a lack of a certain something that makes them 'peculiar.' This is what in fact is meant by a failure of character.[52]

The reason for Nick's break-up with Marjorie becomes clearer in "The Three-Day Blow," the story following "The End of Something." Hamid finds that

it is difficult to describe the exact nature of a man-woman relationship in Hemingway in so far as the women characters are so thinly portrayed that we know but little about them. The male characters, on the other hand, have such gigantic egos that it is not possible for them to achieve any but the most unsatisfactory level of relationship with their women: a relationship of animal attraction or infatuation. Their silly interaction of the need to protect their freedom does not justify their initial need for women. The Hemingway protagonists merely bed women, and are equally keen to share the excitement of the woman's love, but they are largely so full of themselves that they are incapable of responding to their female partners' feelings and sentiments.[53]

"Cat in the Rain" testifies to this deficiency. It is a story about an American couple staying in a hotel in Italy. George, the husband, is completely indifferent to his wife's feelings. As the story progresses, we realize that his wife is pining away for domesticity which he has denied her. George prefers his freedom without the concomitant responsibilities of parenthood and domesticity. He wants the body of his wife without the feminine feelings that normally come with the territory. Perhaps failure in love comes from male-dominated societies, and this is a reason that Indians adore his love stories.

In "Cross-Country Snow," the protagonist Nick Adams regrets his approaching parenthood when his wife, Helen, gets pregnant. In "Hills Like White Elephants," where a man is taking a young woman to Madrid for an abortion, the notion of parenthood is a catastrophe for the Hemingway protagonist. For the woman the child is "everything;" but for the man it means responsibility and loss of freedom. The man cares more about his selfish notion of freedom and less about the woman's feelings about her unborn baby. As Hamid states, "Such callous indifference to the woman's feelings—and in proportion so much self-indulgence in the notion of personal freedom—makes Hemingway protagonists lopsided and psychologically gravely affected."[54]

"Up in Michigan," one of Hemingway's earliest stories, proves this point. Liz's love for Jim includes the sexual aspect, but it comes also with warmth and togetherness. As the story ends, Liz takes off her coat and covers Jim with it to save him from the cold. As Hamid describes,

> It is this attitude of one-sided belligerence that puts the seal of failure on the man-woman relationship in Hemingway right from the start. . . . Any woman who tries to dominate her man, and the man who lets himself be dominated by a woman, arouses Hemingway's scorn. . . . And once a man gave up sovereignty to a woman, that was the end of him.[55]

Throughout his fiction, Hemingway cherishes the notion that if men cannot stay away from women, it would be ideal for men to confine the latter to their stations. If a man is unable to do even this, he is subject to Hemingway's disrespect. Francis Macomber, for example, in "The Short Happy Life of Francis Macomber," was completely under the wings of his wife Margot until the moment he conquers his fear and achieves manhood while hunting buffalo in Africa. Regardless of whether Margot shot her husband, the main point that Hemingway tries to get across in this story is that men who let themselves be henpecked by women are less than men and that the sphere of dominance is the exclusive priority of men and rightfully so. Hemingway heroes are a proud bunch and they regard all dependence on and dominance by women as lacking in their manhood and thus quite unacceptable.

Only in one Hemingway short story, "Fathers and Sons," do we find that the protagonist, Nick Adams, has a satisfying love-relationship with an American-Indian woman named Trudy. But overall, the Hemingway protagonist is unable to comprehend that a love-relationship is a two-way channel that involves give and take, sacrifice and responsibility and that a woman's feelings should be taken into consideration.

Indian readers, on their first reading of the Hemingway short stories, may not get the true nature of man-woman relationships of which Hemingway approves. Indian readers may be inclined to think that Hemingway deliberately makes the woman less than the man and that the woman is subservient to the man. But to blame Hemingway as an insensitive one-dimensional man is to condemn his art. Objective Indian readers, however, would recognize a number of tenets in his concept of love that a very close and careful reading of his short fiction reveals. First, Hemingway wants his readers to focus on the male protagonist in his fiction. This is because the male protagonist has the courage that takes into account physical power, brute force and a corresponding mental freedom from fear. Second, the world of Hemingway is the world of man where the man is guided by the sole yardstick of courage. The woman has neither the scope nor the rightful place in it. Here man single-handedly pursues his manliness without seeking help from woman or without being dependent on her.

Hemingway's own life gives us some clue to an understanding for the failure of love in his short stories. As Hamid observes,

> The gigantic ego of the protagonists who are out to conquer the world does not allow normal emotional links between themselves and their women to be forged. In dealing with their women they are dealing with something they have neither the time nor the inclination to understand. Viewed from a point of view other than theirs, the Hemingway protagonist looks no better than a charlatan, a bit of an anti-hero whose tragedy lies in being forced to play a role for which they have little training and loss of temperament. It is when we read the 'love stories' of Hemingway that we realize the sheer lopsidedness of his heroes. They act and behave like the dropouts of society without realizing that they are dropouts.[56]

Indeed, many Indian characters in Bengali novels and short fiction resemble the Hemingway protagonists. Whether this is because of the nature of the Indian psyche or a desire to identify with the male hero is a debate comparable to the chicken and the egg.

Resignation and Affirmation

Some of Hemingway's short stories deal with his notion of man. These stories record the protagonist's state of mind and behavior in a situation of crisis in his life. For Hemingway it is not the outcome but the manner in which a man faces the situation that is important. We can deduce two sets of reactions and states of mind: one in which a man is driven to the point of soul-weariness where desperate acceptance becomes synonymous with courage, for example, Ole Anderson in "The Killers;" and the other in which the protagonist struggles against heavy odds in the face of defeat and though he may be apparently defeated, like Santiago in *The Old Man and the Sea*, he emerges as the undefeated and his victory lies in the nobility of his struggle. In all of these stories, it is the individual who has to face the trials alone; that is, he has to rely completely on himself. As Hamid notes, in "The Killers," "Resignation or acceptance with dignity becomes synonymous with courage."[57]

If, for Ole Anderson, courage lies in facing his death, for the major in "In Another Country," it lies in facing life despite its emptiness. In some stories, says Hamid, "Hemingway portrays his protagonist in the act of redemption moments before his death, thereby giving some meaning to his otherwise barren life."[58] Harry, for instance, in "The Snows of Kilimanjaro," is a writer who has resigned himself to a life of comfort, wealth and luxury that has resulted in his not being able to utilize his talent for writing. He is very close to death, lying on the hot plains of Africa with a gangrenous leg, knowing that he is going to die, and he makes a desperate attempt to redeem himself. In another story, "The Short Happy Life of Francis Macomber," Hemingway portrays his protagonist in the act of manhood. Long henpecked by his wife Margot, Francis Macomber eventually conquers his fear and achieves manhood while hunting in Africa, but his 'happy life' is cut short by death. This attitude is very meaningful to people whose lives are filled with tragedy and premature death.

In some stories, the Hemingway protagonists are aging professionals—boxers, bullfighters or fishermen—who, despite their age, show tremendous will power by their unwillingness to give up. According to Hamid, ". . . it is their effort to prove themselves despite their limitations that all the more increases their heroic stature. In "Fifty Grand," for instance, the Hemingway protagonist, Jack Brennan, displays extraordinary endurance and courage, the two qualities that Hemingway much admires."[59] In "The Undefeated," the protagonist, Manuel Garcia, is an aging bullfighter who is just out of the hospital after being wounded in a bullfight, but even at this stage he does not want to give up bullfighting. As Hamid observes,

> Hemingway, in this story, has used the bullfight as a means for dramatizing the values he admired, namely courage, endurance, dignity and skill. Like hunting, boxing and fishing, the bullfight has certain fixed rules and moreover, the individual has to rely completely on his inner resources. . . . The Hemingway protagonist asserts himself in the face of tremendous odds and it is his will to struggle that gives him heroic proportions. Even death becomes unimportant in his single-minded pursuit of courage and in his obstinate attempts to prove himself.[60]

In the stories above, I have discussed the themes of resignation and affirmation from the perspectives of Indian readers and critics. According to Hamid,

> These two themes—resignation and affirmation—are in fact two sides of the same coin because they represent two different ways in which the protagonists face their situations, in either case exemplifying the values of courage, endurance and dignity. Hemingway worshipped individual courage and heroism. He had a

romantic notion of man, brave, virile, an eminent macho figure. In these stories, he puts men in situations where they have to rely completely on themselves and the way they face their situations provides the test of highest dignity and highest courage.[61]

Chapter Five:
Hemingway's Novels in Bangladesh

Hemingway's novels are as equally popular and well-received in Bangladesh and India as his short stories. To understand why, we will examine Bangladeshi and Indian perspectives of four of Hemingway's most important and representative novels: *The Sun Also Rises* (1926); *A Farewell to Arms* (1929); *For Whom the Bell Tolls* (1940); and *The Old Man and the Sea* (1952).

The Lost Generation

Although *The Sun Also Rises* was published in 1926, it was first translated and published in Bangladesh in September 1974, shortly after Bangladesh's war of independence in 1971. Translated by Abul Fazl and published by Mowla Brothers, the novel's reception in the late 1970s and early 1980s was quite mixed. According to Kaiser Haque, the bourgeois and conservative critics openly showed their discomfort and displeasure; and together with the fundamentalist mullahs (preachers of Islam) and Hindu priests (who are guardians of the temples), they condemned the novel as inimical to the progress of society. For bourgeois and conservative critics, the novel was a threat to progress because it espoused liberalism and freedom from moral values. All four groups—bourgeois, conservatives, fundamentalist mullahs, and Hindu priests—basically trained their attacks on the characters in the novel who thrive on pointless and seemingly amoral lives. Because of this amoral and free lifestyle, these critics believed the translation and subsequent publication of the novel was unjustifiable. A few went so far as to advocate its ban, comparing it, erroneously enough, with *Fanny Hill* by John Cleland and *Lady Chatterley's Lover* by D. H. Lawrence.[1]

Haque, by the same token, identifies an opposing but very liberal group of critics who often overlook problems of technique and style, but find similarity and common ground between Hemingway's characters, especially in *The Sun Also Rises*, and their own generation. These liberal critics were fascinated by the notion of a lost generation, a literary term now attributed to Gertrude Stein, but introduced by Clifton Fadiman.[2]

Despite the sell-out of the first printing between 1974 and the reprint of the second edition in February 2005, a small but determined number of Bangladeshi critics paid relatively little attention to *The Sun Also Rises*, which many may have had something to do with their prejudices. However, another reason for its under-evaluation is that by the mid-1970s, this novel was regarded as an early introductory work of lesser significance than Hemingway's other major novels. Thus, they concluded that Bangladeshi readers were already familiar with it and paid it little attention.

Although these bourgeois and conservative critics, mullahs, and Hindu priests downplayed the importance of this novel depicting American Bohemians in Paris and Spain in the early part of the twentieth century, and called for its ban because they thought it would escalate moral laxity, this novel's bumpy initial reception paved the way for reading more of Hemingway's novels in Bangladesh, not fewer. As Farzana Akhter, Senior Lecturer in English at East West University, remarks, "I have read *The Sun Also Rises*. At that time, I was so bemused by Hemingway's writing that I wanted to read more."[3] Masrufa Ayesha Nusrat, Senior Lecturer in English at East West University, agrees:

> I read *The Sun Also Rises* in English when I was in Master's level. The novel seemed meaningless when I first read it. But when the teacher explained its context, it seemed to be packed with meaning. Perhaps more reading would provide more inspiration to know about the American culture and society.[4]

Mohammad Tasnim Chowdhury, Lecturer in English at Stamford University in Dhaka, recalled having had a similar experience: "I read *The Sun Also Rises* in my Master's. Probably because it was my text, I failed to enjoy it. From my memory, it really brought Spain to life."[5] Golam Gaus Al-Quader, Lecturer in English at the University of Dhaka, likes *The Sun Also Rises* because of its "reticent treatment of themes," but dislikes it because of its "obsession with the seamy side of life and people."[6] This meager sampling of views suggests this early novel by Hemingway is remembered not for its morally corrupting influences on graduate students but for stimulating a desire to learn and read more.

Others also initially stumbled on a few aspects of *The Sun Also Rises* before appreciating its inner meaning. Nusrat Jahan, Lecturer in English at Primeasia University, recalls reading the novel in English:

> I had to struggle with the diction, which is elliptic, non-sequential, and not-easy-to-follow; and sometimes incomprehensible narrative. The only thing that becomes evident after reading that particular novel is the hero's excruciating yet impotent anger stemming from his physical disability. But I don't agree with the way the hero finds or tries to find or create a meaning out of life and his disabled existence. That seems like a working arrangement.[7]

According to Tahmina Ahmed,

> Except for the ending, *The Sun Also Rises* is a breakthrough novel of the Lost Generation. The ending always makes me feel that Hemingway stopped writing abruptly because he lost interest in his

characters. I also find that apart from Jake and Brett, the other characters are not presented fully and not developed very well. But I also feel that it is a succinct expression of the time and society that it explores: the Lost Generation.[8]

Hemingway received criticism, especially from the gender critics, for not treating the female character with as much sympathy as the male one. As Dr. Firdous Azim, chair of the Department of English at BRAC University in Dhaka, states,

> When I read *The Sun Also Rises*, I thought it was a wonderful novel, upholding the spirit of the Lost Generation in Paris. The Jake Barnes character is portrayed with sensitivity and compassion. However, Lady Brett Ashley does not get the same treatment, and there is something of a misanthrope in Hemingway, which I find disturbing.[9]

Shuchi Karim, Lecturer in English at BRAC University in Dhaka, finds the description of "life and its events" in the novel to be the indelible ink in the minds of Bangladeshi readers. According to Karim,

> It is the color and the vivid description of life and its events that stands out in a reader's mind. It doesn't matter whether the reader is familiar with the concepts of the Lost Generation and 'Nihilism'— the novel captures the 'aimlessness' of youth; 'meaningless' life and a breakaway from structure. There is nothing predictable about life anymore—these are contemporary realities as well. That is why Hemingway and novels like *The Sun Also Rises* stand the test of time.[10]

A similar theme resonates with Tabassum Zaman, Lecturer at BRAC University in Dhaka, who states, "*The Sun Also Rises* captures the cultural and psychological disorder after the First World War. I like the way Hemingway questions the traditional perception of gender and redefines masculinity and femininity through his portrayal of Jake Barnes and Brett Ashley."[11]

Similarly, Dr. Sirajul Islam Chowdhury, former professor of English at the University of Dhaka and an eminent critic, finds that the theme of *The Sun Also Rises* is the "moral plight of postwar expatriates in Paris and Spain."[12] Fakrul Alam agrees: "*The Sun Also Rises* is overwhelming in its portrayal of the Parisian wasteland, and expatriates adrift."[13] Finally, as Dr. Selim Sarwar, associate professor of English at North South University, aptly states, "*The Sun Also Rises* is a period piece—but perhaps the most perfect period piece for that generation."[14]

Zobaida Nasreen, Lecturer in English at Stamford University in Dhaka, calls *The Sun Also Rises* "wonderful writing of Ernest Hemingway," as it impels the lost generation to rise again, like the sun. Nasreen finds that

> this postwar piece fully described the situation and state of the

society after the war such as uncertainty and inconsistency in life. At that time, life was suffering from a sense of rootlessness described through the characters of Jake and Brett. Reflecting the postwar period, this novel has shown that all the characters are floating and showing no respect for each other, which is actually the way to search for roots. But the last page of this piece has shown a positive attitude toward life, and the utter disillusionment is what must impel the Lost Generation—or a future generation—to rise again.[15]

Farzana Zebeen Khan, Lecturer in English at BRAC University in Dhaka, finds a personal connection with *The Sun Also Rises*: "This novel is a wonderfully written saga of a war-wounded person and the postwar period. I especially liked Hemingway's theory of Grace Under Pressure. I believe most of us live according to this theory without knowing it."[16]

Despite this novel's mixed reception by conservative critics, religious leaders and non-conformists, Kaiser Haque writes that

> *The Sun Also Rises* deserves special attention because, besides probably being Hemingway's best novel, it offers the most dramatic and also perhaps the most convincing picture of the code in operation. It has two epigraphs, one of the famous pronouncements of Gertrude Stein on the young expatriates, labeling them as 'a lost generation,' and the other a passage from the Bible declaring that the 'earth abideth forever' though generations come and go in an irrevocable sequence. Hemingway himself has tried to relate the two epigraphs to the novel by saying that the true protagonist is the abiding earth and this serves to refute Stein. But the general view of his readers is that he was wrong. What grips our attention throughout the novel is 'the lost generation' and its partly successful struggle to impose meaning on chaos. Clearly, the sense of the earth providing an eternally stable and vital power, which can rescue the lost generation from the grip of *nada*, is missing. Man, and not nature, is the measure of all things in *The Sun Also Rises*; and man covers a broad spectrum of humanity between the polar opposites of Robert Cohn and Pedro Romero.[17]

From this perspective, Haque further reflects on Jake Barns:

> Between the two stands the protagonist, Jacob or Jake Barnes. He is opposed to Cohn and draws his strength from what Romero stands for. Because of a wound suffered in the First World War, he cannot consummate his sexual desires, which are otherwise quite normal. His exact opposite in this respect is the female protagonist, Lady Brett Ashley, who is leading a phenomenally promiscuous life. The two are as close to being lovers as circumstances permit. The result is that both, but especially Jake, suffer extreme anguish. Jake's response to such agonizing circumstances is to take it not lying down but standing up, without flinching. He keeps self-pity at bay by adopting a hard-boiled stoic attitude, even treating his wounding as a joke. But

when he is alone at night he sometimes breaks down and sobs. As he puts it, 'It is awfully easy to be hard-boiled about everything in the daytime, but at night it is another thing.' Living under such stress, it is all he can do to keep himself from becoming a psychic wreck. In moments of extreme anguish, the existential foundation of the code is laid bare: 'Perhaps as you went along you did learn something. I did not care what it was all about. All I wanted to know was how to live in it, maybe if you found out how to live in it you learned from that what it was all about.' The extremity of Jake's condition, in spite of which he maintains his equilibrium, makes him a convincing character and gives the lie to the notion of the code hero as a naive poseur. He is also capable of genuine sympathy and healthy sentiments as his relationships with Brett and his male friends show; he can sniff a rose without appearing to be a caricature. Jake and his friends form an in-group whose members embody the traits of the code figure in varying degrees. There are minor characters like Harvey Stone, Count Mippipopolous and Harris who make fleeting appearances. . . . Bill Gorton, who comes from America to join the Party to Pamplona, is the most humorous character in the novel. He can view the situation from a comic angle and with a few verbal mannerisms present it before the others in a ludicrous light. Yet, at the same time, he is capable of genuine courage as when he rescues the black boxer from the mob in Vienna. Of the men in the group he is the one with whom Jake feels the most affinity. Then there is the Mike Campbell, Brett's fiancé, a chronic bankrupt always flying from responsibility.

Judged by the code as it emerges in the novel, all these characters are found wanting in one respect or the other. Harvey has the stoicism but it is threatened by increasing bitterness and veiled self-pity. Bill and the Count cannot balance Epicureanism with stoicism, having a bit too much of the former, and Bill's verbal pranks verge too often on escapism through humor and irony. The Count is constantly immersed in the epicurean delight of champagne-drinking. These neat judgments should be taken with a grain of salt. Still, some general evaluation can be made, and has its value, even when it is done by what may be called the 'liquor standard,' that is, by the reaction of people to liquor. As Jake judges, 'Mike was a bad drunk. Brett was a good drunk. Bill was a good drunk. Cohn was never drunk.' Mike falls below Brett and Bill, but stands above Cohn because Cohn does not even dare to let himself go.

The trip to Pamplona brings all the chief characters together and sets the stage for the dramatic presentation of a number of tangled relationships through which the revelation of the code is completed. The in-group, comprising Jake, Brett, Mike and Bill, feel at home in the world and atmosphere of the fiesta; but Cohn is an outsider whose incompatibility with the rest of the party results in constant friction between him and Mike and Bill. He is persistent in his courtship of Brett because he cannot accept the fact that his affair with Brett in San Sebastian means nothing to her. Mike and Bill freely indulge in baiting Cohn, making insidious remarks when not openly baiting him. Cohn's undignified response to Frances's tirade is an index of his unsoundness of character. His alienation from the group and the spirit of the fiesta is brought out with a comic turn in the scene where he passes out in the midst of carousing while the rest continue inebriating themselves and are entirely at one with the festive spirit.

The Brett-Romero affair progresses to its culmination in Madrid. Brett realizes the innocence and simplicity of Romero and her own fallen state and decides not to corrupt him. By sending him away she redeems herself: 'You know it makes one feel rather good deciding not to be a bitch,' she tells Jake. 'It's sort of what we have instead of God.' Here, like Catherine Barkley in the face of death, Brett lives up to the code.

Though the code-hero who receives the most attention is Jake, a purer example is Romero. His life centers completely around bullfighting, and the perfection he exhibits in his art becomes also the index of his moral integrity. The perfect figure he makes in the amphitheatre is precisely described to create a vivid image of the ordering of chaos bullfighting is supposed to demonstrate: 'Each time he let the bull pass so close that the man and the bull and the cape that filled and pivoted a head of the bull were all one sharply etched mass.' This is similar to the image of perfect aesthetic ordering that we find in the famous line from Yeats. 'How can I know the dancer from the dance?' Like Yeats's dancer, Romero is part of a perfect pattern. Leo Gurko neatly points out the difference between the two code heroes in the novel when he writes, 'His (Jake's) heroism, unlike Romero's is not that of consummation but of effort.'[18]

Zerin Alam, on the other hand, finds *The Sun Also Rises* to be a major novel of the 1920s that captures "the nuance of the Jazz Age:"

> Hemingway completes the literary record of the twenties in his depiction of two aspects that are absent in *The Great Gatsby*, which are the after effect of the war and the expatriate theme. *The Sun Also Rises* is about a group of American and British expatriates living in Paris and trying to come to terms with the postwar society. The novel resembles *The Great Gatsby* in its portrait of the dissolute lifestyle of a generation given to drinking and loose morality. In *The Sun Also Rises* the broad contours of the Jazz Age is easily recognizable in Jake and his friends' club hopping, dancing and drinking. The drunken fights at the end of Gatsby's parties are repeated in the bars of the Left Bank of Paris. The cool immoral flapper of New York has a new avatar in Brett Ashley, the bitch goddess who discards her men as soon as she has used them up.[19]

Alam also finds the expatriate theme fully developed in *The Sun Also Rises*, in comparison with F. Scott Fitzgerald's *The Great Gatsby*:

> Hemingway gives *The Sun Also Rises* a powerful symbol of dislocation in the expatriate community in his novel. He connects the theme of the expatriate with the theme of the war by showing that one is a corollary of the other. The Americans living in foreign cities

represent the displaced post-war generation without home and family. Although Nick and Gatsby were both soldiers who had fought in Europe, Fitzgerald does not develop the dilemma of the alienated soldier who returns to a home that is changed. Hemingway like John Dos Passos is a major writer of war fiction and he protests against war when he stresses the after effects of shell shock and violence on men and women.

Jake is a graphic representation of the shell-shocked soldier who is physically and mentally wounded. While Hemingway does not disclose the exact nature of the wound, he insinuates it is a sexual one, which has left Jake impotent. . . . The impotence is symbolic of the breakdown in communication and the fragmentation of modern relationships. Through Jake's castration *The Sun Also Rises* thematically foregrounds (sic) disruption of conventional gender and sexual roles. Thus Jake the main protagonist is impotent and dominated by Brett. Meanwhile Brett is part of postwar feminism with her dominance over the male characters and sexual assertiveness.

Jake's wound, however, goes beyond the physical and social domain to a personal psychological and spiritual crisis. He introduces himself to his companion Georgette as a sick person and she is very understanding because 'Everybody is sick. I'm sick too.' He is also afraid of the dark and there are many instances of his inability to sleep. The bitterness and dissatisfaction following the war is extended to nearly all the characters. Brett Ashley also confesses that all the dancing, drinking and casual relationships have failed to cheer her up and she laments 'Oh, darling, I've been so miserable.' Other glaring evidences of emotional dislocation and angst are the numerous characters who are divorced or rejected by the ones they love and unable to forge new relationships. Brett, for example, has transformed into a bitch who exploits and runs through a series of lovers because the one she loved died in the war. Another major consequence of the war was the inability to readjust to the old pattern of behavior at home. As a result Hemingway's characters in *The Sun Also Rises* and elsewhere reject America for political and social reasons. Jake and his friends choose to live in Paris as Hemingway did himself.

Although *The Sun Also Rises* lacks the romantic glamour and the sentimental prose of *The Great Gatsby*, it is strangely enough the more optimistic of the two novels. In Fitzgerald's novel the plot revolves around the failure of a dream and the narrator leaves New York to return to the staid correctness of the provincial town. The destruction of the dream ends the novel with a terrible sadness and pessimism. In Hemingway's novel, on the other hand, there is no promise of any transcendence or any hint of any idealism. Yet Jake, unlike Carraway, continues to live in the modern social hell in spite of everything. Instead of surrendering or rejecting the social chaos around, Jake makes conscious effort to find salvation. He escapes momentarily from the madness and unhappiness of modern society by going to Spain with its traditional lifestyle and values. In Burguette and Pamplona Jake can reaffirm his faith in mankind and in himself because the combination of male comradeship, sports and natural beauty is (sic) rejuvenating and restorative. Jake can thus develop a personal code of honor based on integrity and self-respect, which permits to maintain grace under pressure in modern society.[20]

The Jazz Age of the 1920s remains an exciting and vivacious time as evidenced by *The Sun Also Rises*, but literary aesthetics of the 1920s gave way to the ideological socialist novels of the 1930s. With the exception of John Steinbeck, many of the writers of this era—Albert Maltz, Albert Halper, Erskine Caldwell, Robert Cantwell, James T. Farrell, and Josephine Herbst—have passed into oblivion. Despite this, Hemingway, Faulkner, and Dos Passos continued to be the major writers of the 1920s and beyond. Of these three, Hemingway comes out on top as the chief spokesman of the 1920s. "Thus," Alam finds, "the swinging band music days of the turbulent roaring twenties was a party that was worth throwing at least for the literature bequeathed to posterity."[21]

Love and Its Conflicts

Although Hemingway became well-known in Bangladesh after the publication and translation of his early short stories and translation of *The Sun Also Rises* in 1974, it was *A Farewell to Arms* (1929) that institutionalized his reputation as a writer of world-importance. *A Farewell to Arms* was translated twice into Bengali and published in Bangladesh. The first translation—by Qamrul Islam—was published in February 1970 and republished in July 2000 by Mowla Brothers in Dhaka. The second translation—by Neaz Morshed—was published in 1988 and republished in 2002 by Sheba Prokashoni in Dhaka. The first printing of the two translations sold out quickly.

Its early success in Bangladesh stems from the novel's anti-war message espoused through a romantic love story between Lt. Frederic Henry and Nurse Catherine Barkley. Pacifists loved the novel because of its stand against war as the destroyer of civilization and humanity; and young readers loved the novel for its love story. No matter which or both were correct, the moral of the story was readily accepted by the general readers as well as the critics.

Although some Bangladeshi scholars griped about the novel's disregard of ethical norms, others recognized Hemingway's remarkable narrative technique. The laudatory statements from critics indicate how strongly the translation was received by a cross-section of the Bangladeshi readers: Khaliquzzaman Elias calls *A Farewell to Arms* "another Hemingway classic."[22] Sirajul Islam Chowdhury calls it "the best novel by Hemingway."[23] Kaiser Haque predicts the novel to be "always popular."[24] "It is such a romantic novel," says Fakrul Alam, "that it is appreciated by both the young and the old."[25] Dr. Deena Forkan, assistant professor of English at North South University in Dhaka, agrees: "*A Farewell to Arms* is a skillfully written love story with admirable characterization."[26] Tahsina Yasmin calls it "a striking piece of literature with the realistic scenario of war and a passionate relationship between the soldier and the nurse.[27,]

Of course, there are also critics who love the novel mainly for its pacifistic, anti-war messages. As Selim Sarwar states, "I value it not only as an anti-war novel, but also as a statement of Hemingway's own take on life."[28] Commenting on the movie version, Mohammad Tasnim Chowdhury had praise for its anti-war content: "I admit that I have not read *A Farewell to Arms*, but I have seen the movie, in fact, both black and white and color versions. The one with Rock Hudson is good, but the one with Chris O'Donnell and Sandra Bullock is better. It was really touching and one of the better anti-war movies I have ever seen."[29]

In addition to the blending of themes of love and war, Resalath Sultana finds many uses of symbols in *A Farewell to Arms*. According to Sultana, "The novel beautifully interweaves love and war. We find the hero involved with both love and war. Hemingway uses a lot of symbols here. But one symbol, rain, which indicates misery, is a matter of surprise to me. It differs with other writers. For example, Coleridge symbolizes rain as a blessing of God or purification. But it is really a heart-breaking novel."[30]

Tahmina Ahmed finds *A Farewell to Arms* to be poetic and lyrical:

> I liked this one more than *The Sun Also Rises* because I found it more poetic and lyrical. It is also structured excellently with each chapter revealing new thoughts about the characters. The description of the love-making is unparalleled. I also found the ending as a natural evolvement of the plot; it ends like a circle, beginning and ending with the figure of the lonely hero on the mountain.[31]

Shuchi Karim makes a connection between the novel's Frederic Henry and Hemingway himself:

> What strikes me most about *A Farewell to Arms* is how close Frederic Henry and Hemingway are as characters. You get a feeling that Hemingway is present in Henry and it gives an authentic (but too close for comfort) feel to the novel. The novel is about love and loss primarily (though the World War looms large) and in the end about acceptance of defeat, and thus 'victory' in defeat. The theme is dominated by magic-incidents and a sense of 'hopelessness,' no matter how hard we fight to live, to get closer to our goals. The truth of life is bitterly projected by Hemingway, that is, we end up defeated, but it is the human power to go on that makes us extraordinary.[32]

Imrana Islam, a faculty member in the English department at Stamford University in Dhaka, finds *A Farewell to Arms* to be a novel of "psychological realism:"

> *A Farewell to Arms* is a tale of the love between ambulance driver Lt. Frederic Henry and Nurse Catherine Barkley during World War I. The action takes place in Italy and the two fall in love during the war

and will stop at nothing to be together. It also analyzes Lt. Henry's feelings on war—the purpose of fighting. Thus it is a novel of psychological realism. Through the character of Frederic Henry, Hemingway eloquently argues against war. Henry accepts what life hands him without murmuring, but argues the fatalist's philosophy: whether you were good or bad, 'they killed you in the end.' Moreover, Hemingway shows how World War I transformed many of those who fought in it into a generation of cynics. Hemingway portrays a sophisticated, intimate and caring relationship between Henry and Catherine, a relationship entered into without the benefit of marriage. But in the end Catherine dies. Consequently, Henry gives a farewell not only to the war but also to his beloved. For Henry, stunned by grief, there was no place to go, nothing to do, no one to talk to. He ambled aimlessly from the hospital through the rainy streets of Lausanne, a broken and lonely man. The novel, in many other ways as well, helped break new social and literary frontiers, with its economical style and emotional understatement.[33]

Based on these critical responses of Bangladeshi readers, scholars and general readers alike broadly lauded *A Farewell to Arms* on two aspects: first, the details of a love story between Frederic and Catherine; and second, the presentation of war as a dehumanizing phenomenon on mankind. Hemingway gives a vivid description of love between the two main protagonists—Frederic and Catherine—and without enumerating the causes of war, shows the impact of war on the bodies and minds of people. We should not blame Frederic Henry for his desertion because it is not typical or representative, but is one person's route to escape.

General readers in Bangladesh recognize that Hemingway's writings do not necessarily showcase a broad picture of society and that many of his characters are people "outside" of society; for example, boxers, bullfighters, and even criminals. Another element that is prominent in Hemingway's novels is alcohol. If living and thriving in water is an enjoyment for fish, then the consumption of alcohol is an enjoyment for the Hemingway characters. Through alcohol, the characters make their suffering endurable and overcome the fear of death. Hemingway's characters also seek relief in love and sex, a view that is shocking for conservatives and mullahs. But most moderates do not attempt to put a cloak of moralistic judgment or condemnation on Hemingway for building his characters the way he did. Based on the love between Frederic Henry and Catherine Barkley, which develops in the midst of the misery of war, they tolerate or accept the way Hemingway has Catherine Barkley submit to Frederic—physically as well as mentally.

The Enemies Within

For Whom the Bell Tolls, Hemingway's novel about the Spanish Civil War, has not yet been translated in Bangladesh. Yet surprisingly, critics and many bilingual readers have read the book in English. In general, they have appreciated it without reservation.—Khaliquzzaman Elias calls the book "yet another classic by Hemingway,"[34] while Kaiser Haque calls the novel "a moving one, but the rendering of Spanish into English reads oddly."[35]—Yet some critics are less enthusiastic. According to Deena Forkan, this book is "not one of Hemingway's best novels."[36] Selim Sarwar finds it to be "less impressive than Hemingway's other major novels. It is also a bit melodramatic."[37]

In exploring the reasons behind this mixed reaction in Bangladesh, one discovers that *For Whom the Bell Tolls* was initially read to encourage political re-education for postwar Bangladesh. For this reason, a number of academic critics emphasize Hemingway's objectivity in dealing with a complex political situation similar to the one that existed in pre-independent Bangladesh. Sirajul Islam Chowdhury finds that *For Whom the Bell Tolls* "has remarkable authenticity," noting that "here Hemingway deals with the Spanish peasantry as well as educated people whose emotions and ideas are complex."[38] Indeed, the novel added to the Bangladeshi political and historical consciousness. The novel is not one of propaganda, for the characters are not embodiments of political ideas, but are acting out their own fates.

Hemingway succeeds in presenting their divided world, a world that forces individuals to make a choice, to declare a "yes" or a "no." In a letter dated December 15, 1925 to F. Scott Fitzgerald, Hemingway succinctly describes the literary potential of war:

> Like me to write you a little essay on the Importance of Subject? Well, the reason you are so sore you missed the war is because war is the best subject of all. It groups the maximum material and speeds up the action and brings out all sorts of stuff that normally you have to wait a lifetime to get.[39]

Hemingway's letter to Fitzgerald succinctly explains his vision of war as a fictional device that has the capability to evoke social reality. Indeed, Hemingway's choice of war as a subject matter and setting for his novels distinguishes Hemingway's writing.

Like the two epigraphs in *The Sun Also Rises*, the title of *For Whom the Bell Tolls* makes reference to an earlier writer to set the stage for Hemingway's meditations on war, in this case a civil war in Spain. As Tahmina Ahmed notes,

> Hemingway writes *For Whom the Bell Tolls*, using the Spanish Civil War but concentrating more on some of the people involved in it, rather than any historical events of the war itself. To reinforce the interest in each man's individual role or fate during war, when death is more of a reality than life, Hemingway attaches an epigram from Donne's *Sermons* in the beginning of the novel: 'No man is an island, intire of it self; every man is a piece of the Continent, a part of the main. . . . any man's death diminishes me, because I am involved in Mankinde; And therefore never send to know *For Whom the Bell Tolls*; it tolls for thee.'[40]

She goes on to say that

> many critics maintain that Hemingway succeeds in re-creating a
> Donnean idea of universal brotherhood in *For Whom the Bell Tolls*.
> Jeffrey Walsh in an essay on the novel represents this popular view
> when he writes: 'The fruition of Jordan's mission is the achievement
> of a group identity, a dawning democratic awareness that enables him
> to shed his sense of loneliness and alienation.'[41]

But it is difficult to discover either "democratic awareness" or shedding of
"alienation and loneliness" in Robert Jordan's brief sojourn with a band of
Spanish guerrillas atop a mountain hideout. We find war bringing a temporary
physical closeness to a group of people engaged in a specific task, but the
divisions within the group according to class, position, gender and ideology
remain as distinct as ever. Instead of becoming part of a bigger whole, a
"Continent," the unity is rather a patchwork quilt stitched to hold on for a brief
passage of time. Hemingway's novel ultimately subverts the idea of Donne's
Sermon and modern man remains an island, if not through completion of self,
certainly through separation from others. The reason behind this isolation of
modern man is the inability of the self to relate to any other self, particularly the
marginalized selves inhabiting the fringes of a war-ravaged, disintegrated
society.

The novel begins with the arrival of Robert Jordan among a group of
Spanish guerrillas for a specific task, that is, to blow up a bridge in support of an
allied attack. Jordan is a heroic figure and his superiority is apparent right from
the beginning. He wins the confidence and admiration of the guerrillas by
exhibiting a thorough knowledge of their horses' health only by glancing at
them. He knows everything that has to be done and exactly how it is to be done.
Simultaneously, he suffers from a sense of impending doom and sees signs in
various events and things. The sense of doom is reinforced when Pilar reads his
palm and drops it in alarm. Pilar does not tell him her vision, and Jordan insists
that he does not believe in the superstition of palm-reading; yet he keeps
wondering about it and asking Pilar about it. Throughout the novel, Jordan
struggles to establish an autonomous and independent self against this sense of a
predetermined fate for himself as well as the Republican cause:

> The guerrilla group that Jordan joins is comprised of people whose
> deep-rooted diversity is united under a fragile bond of patriotism and
> ideology. The group is led by Pablo, but from the outset, the wide gap
> between the leader and his followers is apparent. It is actually Pilar
> who holds these men together. The division within Pablo himself is
> immediately felt by Jordan and he recognizes in this once-upon-a-
> time Republican hero, the signs of defeat, sadness, moral cowardice
> and ultimate ruin. Jordan's analysis of Pablo proves too correct as
> Pablo runs away with the detonators. It is typical of Pablo that he
> returns at the last moment to rejoin Jordan and his band. The other
> Spaniards range between Augustin, the fanatical hater, to Rafael, an

irresponsible gypsy who runs off to kill a rabbit for his dinner instead of guarding their hideout. The other group of guerrillas is the band of El Sordo, who fight separately from these people and meet a futile death on the mountain top with no help from Pablo's band. These people are obviously the marginalized lower-rung of Spanish social hierarchy and whatever social positions they may have enjoyed before the war, these have now been erased. They have been pushed to the periphery of human society and appropriately enough, they live in the mountains, hiding from other humans as animals hide in terror. Amidst these people, a university Lecturer finds very little to share except an ideological fervor, and it is exactly that which creates a tenuous bond between Jordan and Anselmo, his sixty-eight year old Spanish guide. Like Jordan, Anselmo is absolutely devoted to the Republican cause and trusts Jordan implicitly. . . . However, though Anselmo trustingly bares his soul to Jordan, the feeling is not reciprocated by Jordan. He does not view Anselmo as a friend or confidante, though he feels affection for him. Jordan's discussion of the war, the politics or his relationships, are all with his own self, that is, Hemingway uses interior discourse in the form of dialogues between the two selves of Jordan to present such thoughts and arguments. . . . Hemingway uses the interior discourse to convey Jordan's ideas regarding different versions of Communism and Socialism and the Republican revolution and Republican bureaucracy. The interior discourse of Jordan also reveals awareness of his own self-division. Jordan is obviously attempting to create a complete self by reconciling the contradictory aspects of himself, which are presented through the two voices used by Hemingway to portray this division. The two voices argue over his beliefs, his attitudes and even his behavior. 'What were his politics then? He had done now, he told himself. But do not tell anyone else that, he thought. Don't ever admit that. And what are you going to do afterwards? I am going back and earn my living teaching Spanish as before, and I am going to write a true book. I'll bet, he said. I'll bet that will be easy.' Hence, throughout the novel we find his inability to open up and communicate with any other person and he remains the solitary stranger who arrived at their mountain—atop with bags of dynamite and a firm resolve to perform his designated function.[42]

Jordan briefly enjoys his rapport with the two women named Maria and Pilar. But Jordan could not bring his relationship with Maria and Pilar to a fruitful conclusion because of his own superiority complex as well as the inherent contradictions and jealousies in the women themselves. As Ahmed states,

> Though Jordan loves Maria, her role is marginalized by her position in the group as well as by Jordan's and Pilar's treatment of her. Maria repeatedly expresses her desire to unite with Jordan by dissolving their two separate entities. At a moment of intense feeling, Maria voices her desire to be 'exactly the same' as Jordan. But Jordan gives an answer redolent of the Lacanian division between gendered

subjects. He says: 'It is better to be one and each one to be the one he
is.' Obviously, Jordan claims the superiority of the privileged
signifier about which Maria initially made the remark. Jordan not
only claims separateness and difference from Maria, he can also
reject Maria and turn his mind to other things considered more
important by himself. Thus, *For Whom the Bell Tolls* portrays a
group of people who are engaged in a common mission but within
whom there is very little unity. It is a war-ravaged country and war
has revealed that the enemy is not only external but also lies within;
hence the appropriateness of the Spanish War, which was a civil war
fought by its own people. The Spaniards were battling their own
battles as well as participating in a war against the Fascists. But the
Republicans proved weaker than their Fascist foes and Hemingway
reveals some of these weaknesses, as he felt them, in his novel.
Through the various Spanish characters, he revealed the divisions
within themselves; Jordan, coming in from the outside, only helped to
make these divisions more sharply etched. However, Hemingway
shows Jordan also as a disintegrating self who cannot create a whole
out of his fragments. Finally, the foreordained doom occurs—the
bridge is blown up, but Anselmo dies and Jordan is badly wounded.
To avoid capture by the Fascists, the guerrilla band has to leave the
mountains. Jordan performs his last heroic act by persuading Maria to
go to safety with Pablo and Pilar. Jordan stays back to hold off the
enemy for a bit longer until his death. The wheel comes full circle—
Jordan is left supine on the ground as we found him at the beginning
but now he awaits a lonely death. The man came in as a stranger and
he is left to die as the most expendable one, the outsider. Man is after
all an island.[43]

A number of other critics agree with Ahmed that even though Jordan sides
with the Communists, he remains detached from complete commitment to their
cause, that is, he remains committed to neither side. Another paradox critics
point out is that although Hemingway demonstrated a new sense of political
responsibility, he looked upon the war as another sport such as a bullfight; thus,
refusing to take sides. For these critics, this lack of commitment is disturbing
and even dangerous.

Despite the political controversy that *For Whom the Bell Tolls* roused in the
minds of some of the critics, yet another group of critics discovered a sense of
realism in the novel. Hemingway excels in describing violence, such as an
airplane or cavalry attack, through creating dialogue, which expresses the
relevant information accurately. Through creating short, bare-boned dialogue,
Hemingway also reveals the true nature of the speaker, the surroundings, the
suspense, and the sensory perceptions. These critics point to the realism
Hemingway is able to create through his reproduction of dialogue by the use of
Spanish words and idioms, literal translations of Spanish expressions into
English, philological explanations, and Spanish obscenities in the dialogue of
the bandits. They point out that Hemingway also excels in his realistic
descriptions of the intimate physical contacts among his characters, such as his

description of sexual intercourse between Jordan and Maria.

Another group of critics finds a more subtle kind of realism in *For Whom the Bell Tolls* because of the way Hemingway treated the Indians. Hemingway used Indians to develop the secondary characters and to illuminate the mind of the protagonist Robert Jordan. El Sordo, has "a thin-bridged nose like an Indian;" Fernando looks like a "cigar store Indian;" and Pilar has a "heavy brown face with the high Indian cheekbones."

Many Bangladeshi critics consider *For Whom the Bell Tolls* to be a giant leap over his previous fictional works. They agree that the novel advocated the new value of brotherhood that Hemingway expressed through Harry Morgan in *To Have and Have Not*. Another group of religiously-oriented Bangladeshi critics found elements of spirituality that they felt contributed to the new affirmation in *For Whom the Bell Tolls*. Although neither Robert Jordan nor the members of the guerrilla band are orthodox Christians, the novel glorifies the majesty of God and the dignity of man. Hemingway reveals the spiritual side of Jordan's rough band members when they are in the situations during which the reality of war becomes most terrifying. *For Whom the Bell Tolls* has something in common with the Bible because it bears the marks of the creation, the creator, and especially that of the redeemer. Stylistically, the novel provided the religiously-oriented critics of Bangladesh with the combination of the realistic and the transcendent that they looked for. Some of these critics even found traces of the religious or the transcendent in the love story Hemingway develops between Robert and Maria.

Hemingway also provides traces of stoic conduct with which his characters can defy the utter meaninglessness of existence. Faced with certain death, Robert Jordan refuses to commit suicide; and Anselmo holds on to his distaste for killing although it costs him his life. Bangladeshi critics were fascinated by the way in which Hemingway characters respond to death. Very few agreed with Lionell Trilling, who claimed that Hemingway's treatment of death was indirect, thwarted, and sentimental. Because Hemingway makes death a part of life in *For Whom the Bell Tolls*, it is not the actual death but the waiting for death that is the ultimate truth. Unlike the existentialists, Hemingway is more concerned with violent death and thus with direct fear. Occasionally, Hemingway's characters are overcome with feelings of hopelessness and meaninglessness even during the brilliance of daytime. Yet Hemingway's characters, in spite of their feelings of alienation and guilt, do not commit suicide. One can connect with violent death as well as expected and awaited death.

For Bangladeshi critics, the treatment of death in *For Whom the Bell Tolls* poses difficulties that generally stem from the legend of the author himself: that is, the fixed conventional viewpoints that critics have established involving the use of favorite phrases, such as "lost generation," "violence and discipline," "valor and defeat," and "Hemingway's code." Frequently, critics deal with the function of death in the works of Hemingway, rather than the manner in which he presents it. They personally recognize the message he is displaying beyond his conventional themes.

Although *For Whom the Bell Tolls* has not yet been translated into Bengali, the critics and educated general readers have welcomed the original in English for reading and reviewing. They have praised the book for its powerful sense of realism, political ideas, spiritual messages, treatment of war and death, existentialism, and passion and love, exemplified by Robert Jordan and Maria. It is hoped that a Bengali translation of *For Whom the Bell Tolls* will help thousands of readers in Bangladesh to enjoy reading one of the most exciting novels of the Spanish Civil War by Ernest Hemingway, the master storyteller of the world.

Man in Nature

Of all of Hemingway's works, *The Old Man and the Sea* (1952) received the highest critical acclaim in Bangladesh as in the rest of the world. Deena Forkan calls *The Old Man and the Sea* "one of Hemingway's best—depicting the essential Hemingway code in all its assets or forms."[44] Almost all Bangladeshi academic critics and general readers lauded its short, sparse, and terse language, its compactness, and its simple but powerful theme. Some critics drew parallels between it and *Across the River and into the Trees* (1950) and Herman Melville's *Moby Dick*. For the most part their criticism focused either on Santiago, whom they believed was the new Hemingway hero representative of the modern age, or on the metaphysical implications of the man versus nature conflict.

Nearly all Bangladeshi academic critics and general readers find that Hemingway's heroes operate on many levels. On a broader level, man is confronted with imminent death or defeat. In the early works, Hemingway's hero usually remains alive at the end. It would be imprudent to have him killed because in the case of Frederic in *A Farewell to Arms*, he has nothing left after his wife and child perish. In the case of Jake Barnes in *The Sun Also Rises*, his impotency has been stressed from the outset. In the later fiction, the hero dies at the end with justifiable, good reason. The matador in "The Undefeated" and the colonel in *Across the River and into the Trees* have contact with their surroundings, and they long for nothing more. The others—Robert Jordan, Harry Morgan, or Francis Macomber—have grasped the ultimate insight of which they were capable and could not exceed this in future life.

But Santiago of *The Old Man and the Sea* is a hero of a different mettle. Although he suffers defeat as completely as the heroes above, the way he accepts it and continues to live demonstrates something that no other Hemingway hero has done or is capable of doing. He is the only Hemingway hero who is capable of the statement, "A man can be destroyed but not defeated."[45] As Khaliquzzaman Elias states, "The 'Grace under pressure' theory can be seen treated successfully in this novel. The old man can be destroyed but not defeated."[46]

Tahmina Zaman Godhuli finds that "because Santiago is an archetype, he is not especially 'life-like,' but nevertheless he is the supreme Hemingway hero and is definitely much more carefully developed than Cantwell, the hero of *Across the River and into the Trees.*"[47] Tahsina Yasmin echoes Godhuli, noting that "Santiago is the embodiment of the Hemingway hero because of his perseverance. Santiago represents man's lonely existence in the world and his eternal struggle for survival."[48]

Sirajul Islam Chowdhury finds heroism in resisting surrender: "The old man who refuses to surrender is a representation of struggle and strength. The novelist has deep understanding of the man and his efforts. The relationship among the man, the fish and the boy is unforgettable."[49]

Firdous Azim calls *The Old Man and the Sea* "a work of man against nature as well as man in nature. It is a study of endurance, an examination of strength and manliness, but because it is done through an old man, it has become a beautiful portrait of maturity and resilience."[50] Farhana Yasmin Jahan, a faculty member in the English department at Dhaka College in Dhaka, concurs:

> *The Old Man and the Sea* is a detailed story of an old man who fights against powerful nature with what little effort he has. But he faces this indomitable nature with courage without fearing it. With great courage and endurance he faces the fierce forces of nature. He fights with the sharks—a symbol of veritable death—of the sea, and survives.[51]

As a young girl, when Tahmina Ahmed first read *The Old Man and the Sea*, she found it "a bit repetitious and boring." Years later, when she reread it as a graduate student, she could appreciate "the bare and sparse style . . . [and] admired the old man and his gritty determination."[52]

Farzana Zebeen Khan had a similar reaction:

> When I first read it I got bored. But as I grew up I understood the zeal and the passion of the story. The courage to face death with such dignity and to throw challenge in the face of nature could only be depicted by Hemingway's simple but deceptive style.[53]

A sense of the epic proportions of this novel was noted by several interviewees. Nusrat Jahan recalls being moved by the novel's imagery:

> I have read the Bengali version and have seen the film more positively. I do appreciate the struggle of the old man Santiago against the odds, but I failed to valorize it somehow. I, however, liked the loneliness of the human represented through the struggle of the old man and his physical alienation set against a backdrop of the vast, cruel sea. This is the prime image that moved me and made me remember this particular piece of epic.[54]

Masrufa Ayesha Nusrat found it absorbing: "I read *The Old Man and the Sea* in Bengali. I was too young to evaluate it critically. But I remember it to be very absorbing; it gave me a kind of epic feeling of human life."[55] Finally, Selim

Sarwar found the novel's epic proportions surpass the story: "What I find most amazing in *The Old Man and the Sea* is the contrast between its limited scope (in terms of the setting and the number of characters) and the sheer immensity of its message which rivals that of the great classics in fiction such as *War and Peace.*"[56]

In Bangladesh, three different Bengali translations of *The Old Man and the Sea* have appeared. The late, celebrated film actor Foteho Lohani did the first translation, but its publisher and publication date are unknown. Ahmad Mazhar did the second translation, which was published by Student Ways in Dhaka in February 1996. Raoshan Jamil did the third translation, which was initially published by Sheba Prokashoni in Dhaka in November 1987 and subsequently by Projapoti Prokashoni in Dhaka, a subsidiary of Sheba Prokashoni, in February 1993. Needless to say, the first printing of these translations sold out.

Writing in Bengali in the foreword to his translation, Ahmad Mazhar gives the highest credit to Hemingway for his skillful use of short, sparse, and declarative sentences. According to Mazhar, "In his works, Hemingway has used a language that is economical, unpretentious, simple and restrained. He has been able to achieve a unique rhythm through the use of deceptively simple diction."[57] Translator Raoshan Jamil agrees with Mazhar in this respect, stating that "Hemingway's greatest credit lies in his adroit use of language."[58] But in addition to the author's use of language, there is more to *The Old Man and the Sea* that makes it a modern-day epic. According to Jamil,

> To realize his dreams man struggles his best; and often in doing so, he has to subvert the universal laws. Thus the rigors of nature befall him, but he does not yield or give up, and despite the heavy penalty, he establishes his challenge. This is the deepest truth of the mankind that Hemingway strove to illuminate in *The Old Man and the Sea.*[59]

Still, for some critics, Hemingway's final book is one of "contradictions" as well as "masculine vulnerability." As Shuchi Karim states,

> I read *The Old Man and the Sea* in Bengali. . . . It was supposed to be 'the book' to read while growing up. Probably because of such a young age, I found it extremely boring as nothing much happens! Nevertheless, there was something about the book that could even influence my young restless mind to hang-on till the end (probably the old man's character had something to do with it). Like many of Hemingway's other books, there is something depressing about it as well. There are many contradictions present in the book—in the relation between and with man and nature; and within man himself. The book has a 'masculine' vulnerability to it, which I find very interesting: heroism, manhood, and pride are given new names or definitions.[60]

Sayma Arju believes that the old man Santiago is our ideal hero; we look to him as we fight for our survival each day:

The Old Man and the Sea really haunts me still now though I read it about six or seven years ago. I bought the book from a book fair and out of my personal interest I read it. I liked most the protagonist, the old fisherman's character who struggled throughout his life. The description of the sea around him is as wide as his own mind: the atmosphere made him more adventurous. I can even see in front of me the wide sea during sunset when I close my eyes. His struggle was not only with the sharks around his boat, but also with his own ability and his old age. We, the general people, are also doing so. Sometimes we remain conscious about it and sometimes we are not, but the fact is the same; the eagerness of our heart is same. The last part of the novel seemed to me more pathetic. I really feel for the old man, but I think at least he could place a proof or symbol of his work in front of his mates that most of us cannot do throughout our lives. Therefore he has to feel proud for accomplishing his own deed.[61]

There appears to be a common thread between both the Bangladeshi and American reactions to *The Old Man and the Sea*; that is, the old man is less than old but definitely more than man to be called a hero of epic proportions. Both the Bangladeshi and American critics de-emphasize Hemingway's technical sophistication, but attach great importance to his treatment of the mythological, archetypal, and legendary overtones in Santiago's struggle with the fish. Bangladeshis are united in their belief that Hemingway has created a masterpiece in *The Old Man and the Sea*. In Santiago, they have not only found a new Hemingway hero, but also an instructive model for contemporary man. Admittedly, Santiago is less adventuresome outwardly than Hemingway's other heroes, but he makes up for this with his ever-increasing faith in humanity, his humility, and his indomitable spirit. Bangladeshi critics and general readers found the plain, intelligible language of Santiago in accord with the simple but powerful theme of the novel, and perfectly suited to an uneducated fisherman, much like an uneducated fisherman in Bangladesh. Santiago must contend with death and defeat, but his struggle, like that of a fisherman in Bangladesh, is considered more meaningful than that of other Hemingway heroes; for it is not a sought-after quest or adventure, but a part of his daily life and necessary struggle for survival.

Chapter Six:
Hemingway's Novels in India

Turning from Bangladesh to India, how do Indian academic critics and general readers receive *The Sun Also Rises*, *A Farewell to Arms*, *For Whom the Bell Tolls*, and *The Old Man and the Sea*? A key to their critical reaction begins with their insight into the context of the novels—and their interpretations of the meaning Hemingway intended to convey—and extends to the text itself.

The Cycle of Life

Indian scholars and general readers give a thorough and in-depth look at the title of Hemingway's *The Sun Also Rises* before they make an aesthetic judgment on the entire text. In the case of Hemingway's first novel, its title is derived from the Bible, and the relevant passage from Ecclesiastes reads thus:

> One generation passeth away, and another generation cometh; but the earth abideth forever.... The sun also ariseth.... This wind goeth toward the south, turneth about unto the north; it whirleth about continually, and the wind returneth again according to its circuits.... All the rivers run into the sea; yet the sea is not full; unto the place from whence the rivers come, thither they return again.[1]

As the literary scholar Bhim S. Dahiya explains,

> For our purpose, it is the context of *The Sun Also Rises* which is all important. It is therefore necessary here that we remind ourselves of the context in which Hemingway chose to use this passage as the second epigraph to his novel, acting as a kind of counterpoint to the first epigraph.[2]

The first epigraph to the novel reads, "You are all a lost generation." The term *lost generation* was used by Gertrude Stein in her conversation with Hemingway and can also be misleading unless we understand it in the context in which Stein used it to refer to Hemingway's generation. But we can certainly appreciate the novel without relying heavily on the Stein quote. According to Dahiya,

> All the same, the quotation is as useful as an analogy: it clarifies the

idea and has an added charm of its own. Therefore, even though we use the background material as a source of information about the novel's title and theme, for a proper appreciation of the work we must rely on the internal evidence alone.[3]

Some non-Indian critics suggest that the moral of the novel is derived also from the Ecclesiastes: "All is vanity and vexation of spirit."[4] But Indian critics, including Dahiya, disagree:

> Hemingway's novel does not seem to subscribe to such a dogmatic view of life. The novel does, however, try to capture a haunting sense of life's transition, which the experience of war did impart to Jake and his generation—the 'lost generation.' Rather than have a sense of life as 'vanity,' Hemingway's characters carry a dread of death. Unlike the religious people, they try to cling to life rather desperately; for them, life is not a 'vanity,' but a 'feast' where the last course is always death.[5]

Here is a relevant conversation between Robert Cohn and Jake Barnes that borders on death:

> 'Listen, Jake,' he leaned forward on the bar. 'Don't you ever get the feeling that all your life is going by and you're not taking advantage of it? Do you realize you've lived nearly half the time you have to live already?'
>
> 'Yes, every once in a while.'
>
> 'Do you know that in about thirty-five years more we'll be dead?'
>
> 'What the hell, Robert, I said. What the hell.'[6]

We notice Jake's reaction to the mention of death by Cohn as Jake is terrified by the idea of life's impermanence. Characters in the novel resort to different last-ditch solutions because they are plagued by the fear of death. As Mike takes to drinking and the Count to sex, Cohn tries to escape into "romantic" places and "romance" books. Jake advises Cohn that "going to another country does not make any difference," that he has "tried all that," and that "you can't get away from yourself by moving from one place to another."[7] As Dahiya observes,

> More than any other character in *The Sun Also Rises*, it is Jake who is haunted by an acute sense of the impermanence of life, which he carries with him as much in Pamplona as in Paris. This sense of life's transitory nature is conveyed through the recurrent imagery of feast that always ends with empty glasses and mopping-off of tables. . . . As the feast ends in empty glasses, so does life in death.[8]

In *The Sun Also Rises*, even the fiesta at Pamplona becomes a metaphor of this image of life. And as long as the fiesta in Pamplona continues, Jake is able to downplay the haunting sense of life's impermanence because it means "something doing all the time."[9] But as soon as the fiesta is over, he is again taken over by a feeling of emptiness. As Dahiya says, "Feast and fiesta are used as running analogies to life in the novel."[10] Thus, the generation of Jake, Cohn, and Mike as well as of Hemingway, seems to be "lost." Like the sun, it has gone down in that it is facing depression and disillusion. But, as Dahiya explains,

> The fact that he (Hemingway) prefers to entitle it *The Sun Also Rises* clearly shows that he intended to convey not so much the 'lostness' of a generation as its 'rising'—rising out of depression and despair, out of its temporary 'lostness.' . . . The story of Jake Barnes, the hero of *The Sun Also Rises*, is a story of development from a state of chaotic emotions caused by the shock of war to a state of control and discipline over those emotions.[11]

Indian critics disagree with Western critics who view the novel as a static picture of the modern "wasteland," of "vanity," of "futility," or "sterility." Evidently, these critics regard Jake a representative of the sterile land, the wasteland; he is viewed as a spokesman of the lost generation, a sun gone down, never hoping to rise again. According to Dahiya,

> All this is contrary to the textual evidence. The novel clearly dramatizes the development of Jake and Brett, which is the central concern of the novel (sic). In the beginning, we find that emotionally Jake is rather messy, troubled by Brett's inconstancy and yet not being able to detach himself from her. Since Jake has been made a sexual cripple by the war, he cannot satisfy Brett. And Brett, being what she is, cannot help going to other men. What Jake needs to learn, therefore, is to be able to live with, or to overcome the consciousness of, his physical deficiency and to love Brett without the desire to possess her, both of which he gradually attains through a continuous struggle with his own weaker self. His curve of development is, therefore, from the position of 'sun down' to that of 'sun rise.'[12]

This is evident if we notice the plot movement in *The Sun Also Rises*. In the early section of Book I, Jake is always helplessly clinging to Brett and keeps asking her, "Couldn't we live together, Brett? Couldn't we just live together"?[13] However, as we move from Book I to Book II, we find that Jake is no longer the helpless lover he was in Book I; he is trying to stay detached from Brett. As the fiesta in Pamplona comes to an end, so does Book II, the major section of the novel. In Book III, which is only one short chapter, the expatriates start back for Paris. According to Dahiya, this journey from Pamplona to Paris may have been fruitless for Cohn and Mike, who lack 'discipline' and remain 'lost,' but not so for Jake and Brett, who expose themselves to the new setting as they do to every experience of life and are greatly transformed in the process. The last scene, where Jake and Brett are traveling in a taxi in Madrid, is not a repetition of the taxi scene in Paris. . . . If we examine the two taxi scenes closely, it becomes clear that the last taxi scene is not a repetition of the taxi scene at the novel's beginning; rather, the writer has purposely introduced the last taxi scene to highlight the change that comes about the relation between Jake and Brett.

There are in fact two taxi scenes. In the first, Jake craves Brett's body and seems unable to accept the fact that he cannot be Brett's lover. In the second, there are no descriptions of Brett's body, nor any hopeless clinging of the lovers in the darkness of the night; rather, it is a hot and bright day, and the lovers are sitting together without any tension. Further, while the taxi in the first scene goes 'down' the street in the darkness, in the second, it moves 'up' the street in the clear daylight. In other words, while the first taxi scene symbolizes the 'sun-setting' of the lovers, the second symbolizes their 'sun-rising.' The relevance of the novel's title is quite obvious here. There is, therefore, a marked development in the novel from a position of 'the sun-goes-down' to that of 'the sun-also-rises.'[14]

Dahiya also compares Jake and Brett's journey from Paris to Pamplona and back to a similar journey in Shakespeare's *As You Like It*,

where the major characters move from the court to the country and again return to the court. In both cases the strategy behind the juxtaposition is the same: to expose the limitations and virtues of the two places representing the two ways of life and to suggest a new possibility in the reintegration of these separated components of life. Also, the reintegration in both Hemingway and Shakespeare is achieved by the central figures who have the capacity to combine the virtues of the two ways of life. While Shakespeare's heroes and heroines are persons of consequence on whom depends the destruction or reconstruction of order in the entire society, Hemingway's central characters are modern isolates who destroy or reconstruct their own personalities. As we see them at the end of the novel, both Jake and Brett have clearly set their houses in order. The climax in the development of both the characters reaches in their ability to 'discipline' their desires indicated by their acts of self-denial; as Jake denies himself the desire to possess Brett, so does Brett let go Romero whom she so much wanted to possess. Thus, the novel clearly demonstrates that at least Jake and Brett are no longer 'lost' at the end of the novel. They do experience in the novel's beginning a temporary 'lostness'. But while others like Mike and Cohn remain permanently lost, Jake and Brett succeed in disciplining their chaotic emotions. Hemingway's 'lost generation' is therefore not actually lost; it is only as much lost as any other generation. Also, as in the case of other generations, only those of its members are lost who lack self-discipline. Now, the reason why Jake is not totally lost is because he is the only character in the novel who is committed to the values of duty and personal relationship—the two sources of strength which sustain him through the trying experiences of life.[15]

The Sun Also Rises cannot, therefore, be viewed as a social documentation of a lost generation. The novel clearly demonstrates that there is no such thing as a lost generation. Dahiya goes on to say that, far from being "lost,"

> Jake Barnes is the real hero of the novel, who offers a viable response to the challenges of modern life. He is not an 'innocent,' but an 'initiate'—one who has the capacity to expose himself to any new experience of life and has also the capacity to absorb that experience. . . . Hence he is not lost. . . . Thus, the novel's title embodies the novel's theme; *The Sun Also Rises* because the sun contains within itself the energy that sustains. Jake and Brett, as also the generation they represent, rise because they as well as the generation they represent have within them the powers of regeneration; the lasting powers, that is, of human love and endurance. Like any other generation the generation of the twenties feels paralyzed in the face of new challenge; it does temporarily feel lost when it is suddenly cut off from the past quite like a child feels lost when it is weaned away from the mother's breast. But eventually, the generation of the twenties faces the new challenges, acquires a new outlook, and succeeds in adjusting itself to the changed world.[16]

Not only does Dahiya find human love, endurance and regeneration as the hallmark of *The Sun Also Rises*, but also he finds some elements of humor and satire permeating the novel on the sideline. Of course, Hemingway was not an original comic genius in the great tradition of Mark Twain; he carefully adapted his comic elements from both American and British authors, such as Ring Lardner, Mark Twain, and Henry Fielding. Besides Lardner and Twain, he showed affinity with Fielding, the great English comic genius and the father of the English novel, in *The Torrents of Spring*, his first novel. Despite his adaptations of Lardner and Fielding, his respect and admiration of Twain, and his own humorous writings of his school days, most Western critics have seldom paid attention to the element of humor in his major fiction. Hemingway finds no place in the comic imagination of American literary tradition. Nonetheless, Dahiya observes, "I do not of course mean to suggest that most Hemingway novels are comedies. I do, however, want to assert that novels like *The Torrents of Spring*, *The Sun Also Rises*, and *Islands in the Stream* are not without the element of humor."[17]

That *The Sun Also Rises* is a satirical comedy is established by the very opening paragraph of the novel:

> Robert Cohn was once middleweight boxing champion of Princeton. Do not think that I am very much impressed by that as a boxing title, but it meant a lot to Cohn. He cared nothing for boxing, in fact he

disliked it, but he learned it painfully and thoroughly to counteract the feeling of inferiority and shyness he had felt on being treated as a Jew at Princeton. There was a certain inner comfort in knowing he could knock down anybody who was snooty to him, although, being very shy and a thoroughly nice boy, he never fought except in the gym. He was Spider Kelly's star pupil. Spider Kelly taught all his young gentlemen to box like featherweights, no matter whether they weighed one hundred and five or two hundred and five pounds. But it seemed to fit Cohn. He was really very fast. He was so good that Spider promptly overmatched him and got his nose permanently flattened. This increased Cohn's distaste for boxing, but it gave him a certain satisfaction of some strange sort, and it certainly improved his nose. In his last year at Princeton he read too much and took to wearing spectacles. I never met any one of his class who remembered him. They did not even remember that he was middleweight boxing champion.[18]

Needless to say, this is an excellent piece of comic writing. But Hemingway's comic writing is different from that of others. According to Dahiya, "The satirical humor of *The Sun Also Rises* is very much in the mid-Western tradition of humor. Being a mid-Westerner, Hemingway was very much rooted in that tradition. He might have been a great admirer of Mark Twain, but his comic spirit was very different from that of the Southwestern (or frontier) tradition of humor to which Twain belonged."[19]

One comic device that Hemingway has employed effectively is the repetition of a certain phrase or sentence like a refrain. To make the repetition look natural, he generally puts it in the mouth of a drunk. He has quite extensively used this device in *The Sun Also Rises*. On several occasions, the count, Wilson-Harris, Mike, and Bill are used as agents of comedy; they are generally drunk and get stuck to something—an idea, object or expression—and keep repeating it. Here is an example:

> 'You ought to write a book on wines,' count, I said.
>
> 'Mr. Barnes,' answered the count, 'all I want out of wines is to enjoy them.'
>
> 'Let's enjoy a little more of this,' Brett pushed her glass forward. The count poured very carefully. 'There, my dear. Now you enjoy that slowly, and then you can get drunk.'
>
> 'Drunk? Drunk?'
>
> 'My dear, you are charming when you are drunk.'
> 'Listen to the man.'
>
> 'Mr. Barnes,' the count poured my glass full. 'She is the only lady I have ever known who was as charming when she was drunk as when she was sober.'

'You haven't been around much, have you?'

'Yes, my dear. I have been around very much. I have been around a very great deal.'

'Drink your wine,' said Brett. 'We've all been around. I dare say Jake here has seen as much as you have.'

'My dear, I am sure Mr. Barnes has seen a lot. Don't think I don't think so, sir. I have seen a lot, too.'[20]

Dahiya notes, "This is delightful conversation. The way the count and Brett pick up words like 'enjoy,' 'drink,' 'around' and 'seen' and use them repeatedly makes the conversation of drunks humorous. The Count Mippipopolous is not the only agent of comedy in the novel. There are several other minor characters who are largely there for the sake of comedy."[21]

As a satirist, Bill Gorton does not confine his attacks on Parisians alone. He has a wide range of subjects to satirize. He satirizes wherever he goes and whatever he talks about. "But," says Dahiya, "while the drunken tongue makes the narration humorous, the social conscience makes it satirical. The white chauvinism displayed at the prize-fight is quietly exposed by the satirist. Another time, when Jake and Bill are traveling by train in France, Bill again plays the role of satirist and exposes corruption in social life."[22]

There is yet another type of humor in *The Sun Also Rises* that is the verbal humor that emanates from the contrasts of different tongues. Because many of Hemingway's novels, including *The Sun Also Rises*, deal with European situations, they are replete with characters from different nationalities—American, British, French, and Spanish. Befittingly, these different nationalities can speak in a common language even though they speak in their respective tongues. This creates humor, and an example of this type of humor is Jake's conversation with the proprietress of the Hotel Montana in Madrid where Brett is staying after the fiesta is over in Pamplona. Being financially broke, Brett dispatches a telegram to Jake, who at once reaches Madrid and inquires at the hotel about her:

'Muy buenos,' I said. 'Is there an Englishwoman here? I would like to see this English lady.'

'Muy buenos. Yes, there is a female English. Certainly you can see her if she wishes to see you.'
'She wishes to see me.'

'The chica will ask her.'

'It is very hot.'

'It is very hot in the summer in Madrid.'

'And how cold in winter.'

'Yes, it is very cold in winter.'

'Did I want to stay myself in person in the Hotel Montana?'

'Of that as yet I was undecided, but it would give me pleasure if my bags were brought up from the ground floor in order that they might not be stolen. Nothing was ever stolen in the Hotel Montana. In other fondas, yes. Not here. No. The personages of this establishment were rigidly selected. I was happy to hear it. Nevertheless I would welcome the upbringal of my bags.'

'The maid came in and said that the female English wanted to see the male English now, at once.'

'Good,' I said. 'You see. It is as I said.'

'Clearly.'[23]

This conversation between Jake and the proprietress employs certain comedic devices: part of the conversation is directly reproduced, and the rest is reported by the narrator who is Jake himself. This is a bilingual humor of Hemingway vintage at its best. Certainly the fact that this humor is placed before the somber reality of Brett's insolvency heightens the dialogue.

A good number of the Indian reading public may be financially ill-situated, often ill-fed or underfed; but they are intellectually astute enough to find and rejoice in the humor and satire illustrated above and woven through the pages of *The Sun Also Rises*. The aesthetic values of the ancient Indians as well as the moderns have always been sublime when it boils down to appreciating the lighter moments in a great piece of literature such as this.

A Crisis of Meaning

If *The Sun Also Rises* (1926) is the first great novel by Hemingway, most Indian scholars and the general readers regard *A Farewell to Arms* (1929) as his second. As Ramji Lall declares, "Success in fictional craftsmanship and in portraying the mind of an era was again achieved in *A Farewell to Arms*, the poignant love-story of an English nurse and an American ambulance lieutenant during the war."[24] Besides calling the novel a success, Lall goes on to say that *A Farewell to Arms* is complex: "As with *The Sun Also Rises*, the appeal of the book is complex; it interests not only by its love-story, but also by its passages of swiftly paced action, by its expression of the mood of overwhelming revulsion against war which lasted into the nineteen-thirties, and by the overwhelming actuality of its chapters on the rout of the Italian army."[25]

Although there were a number of shocked critical reactions to the initial serialization of *A Farewell to Arms* in *Scribner's Magazine*, Indian readers welcomed the novel. General Indian readers love the novel as well as its movie version for what it is: a love-story of the 1920s in the Romeo and Juliet vein with an anti-war message. These readers also find the novel to be one of a tragedy of aimlessness succeeded by a tragedy of broken hopes.

Yet there are others—general readers, professional critics, university and college faculty, and Hemingway buffs—who view the novel from perspectives ranging from love and war to politics, suspense, humanism, the search for identity, realism, and existentialism. In discussing the themes of love and war and politics, Arindam Dasgupta, a research scholar in the Comparative Literature department at Jadavpur University in Kolkata, West Bengal, finds a vortex of contemporary politics of war and love in the novel. According to Dasgupta, "In *A Farewell to Arms*, the stormy situation of contemporary politics and war is placed side by side with love and eternity, which reminds me of the famous speech of Hemingway that a good enough writer must face eternity, or the lack of it, each day."[26] Indranil Mitra, who teaches at South Point High School in Kolkata, calls the novel a love story that has an autobiographical source. Mitra notes that

> it is a wartime love story between an American ambulance driver named Fredric Henry and an English nurse named Catherine Barkley. Perhaps the story is partially autobiographical, for Hemingway himself had worked as an ambulance driver during the First World War in France and also in Italy.[27]

Overlaying a more realist perspective on love and war, Sayantan Dasgupta, lecturer in Comparative Literature at Jadavpur University in Kolkata, describes the novel as "a triumph of the realist mode of narrative and a convincing anti-war tract."[28] Dr. Sobha Chattopadhya, professor of Comparative Literature at Jadavpur University in Kolkata, agrees:

> Written in the realistic mode, *A Farewell to Arms* is a novel about war and love. The protagonist Fredric Henry is again a 'code hero' standing for courage and endurance. Fighting against feelings of terror, anxiety, evil and darkness that threaten to devour him, he is once again at the center of a parable about the heroic capabilities of man.[29]

Others relate *A Farewell to Arms* to existential concerns. Uma K. Alladi finds strains of existentialism from the smallest to the largest details:

> The death of the ants on the log emphasizes the death experience and a concomitant sense of absurdity in *A Farewell to Arms*. The physical wound, at first, and finally the death of Catherine, make Henry an individual. Just before Catherine's death, he is seized by fear and trembling, seized with fear that she might die. . . . At her death, he is full of despair and disillusionment. He is alone and tormented but

'very much alive in the existential sense.' Henry is a non-croyant,
believing in God only at night."[30]

Dr. Satyabrata Das concurs: "*A Farewell to Arms*, very much like *The Sun Also
Rises* and "In Our Time," deals with the crisis of existence, of survival in a
hostile world."[31]

Hemingway maintains the element of suspense throughout the novel,
according to Dr. J. P. Tripathi of the English department at Gorakhpur
University in Gorakhpur. Comparing it with *The Sun Also Rises*, Tripathi
observes that

> suspense is maintained regarding the love and the future possibilities
> of life between Jake and Brett till at the end there is a clear statement
> that the possibility of a future life between the two does not exist. In
> *A Farewell to Arms* we keep thinking that Catherine might live
> happily together in the future but at the end Catherine is dead.[32]

Sanjukta Dasgupta discusses *A Farewell to Arms* as a work of realism
alongside *For Whom the Bell Tolls* and *The Old Man and the Sea*. According to
Dasgupta believes that both external or objective reality and subjective reality
are present in *A Farewell to Arms*. External or objective reality refers to the
world of phenomena outside subjective thought-processes of an individual.
Subjective reality represents the perceptional world of the human mind.
Subjective reality may include an individual's perceptions, reactions and
realizations, which are derived from an interaction with the objective reality. As
Dasgupta writes,

> In *A Farewell to Arms* the two levels of reality are seen to exist in
> hostile interaction. The objective reality in the novel is the external
> world represented by the war environment and its concomitant
> circumstances. The subjective reality is the perceptional world, as
> observed in Fredric Henry's private world of lost illusions, his love
> for Catherine, his sense of happiness with her and his sense of despair
> when he loses her.[33]

Reality sets in for Fredric as he continues to struggle with fact that he is
now alone and will have to live alone without his beloved. The death of
Catherine has diminished him and made him an emotional wreck. As Dasgupta
notes,

> In *A Farewell to Arms*, love had initially seemed to be a positive
> strength-generating source till tragedy set in and love was destroyed.
> So the final impression derived from the novel is one of unrelieved
> tragic gloom and resignation wherein love is forced to succumb to the
> impersonal forces of the external world. Love, which had initially
> seemed to be of sustaining value, is remembered with too much pain
> and unhappiness as the novel concludes.[34]

Dasgupta finds that *A Farewell to Arms*, among others, contributes significantly in shaping Hemingway's own idea of reality:

> First, Hemingway becomes aware that the individual cannot survive in isolation and is ultimately helpless, despite possessing courage, strength and skill. Love appears as just a temporary oasis preyed upon by the swiftly advancing sands of nothingness. The conclusion that Hemingway deduces is that the individual is part of the human world in totality. But this realization is more asocial and does not necessarily imply a return to human society and its routine activities, thereby leading a life of the Babbits. Personally too, Hemingway preferred to live in the comparative unspoiled natural and secluded environment of Cuba, entertaining friends and relatives occasionally in his spacious villa, rather than living and participating in the social life of New York or any other metropolis for that matter.[35]

Dasgupta discerns that the changes that occur in Hemingway's novels take place in the world of human sensibility:

> The external world of caprice, cruelty and violence remain changeless. The sole moment when a unified aesthetic impression is gained is when the barriers between the external world and the perceptional world of the individual melt into each other. This occurs when the protagonist makes an effort to overcome the ruthless circumstances, though aware of the fact that he has engaged himself in an unequal struggle. Nevertheless, he participates in such a struggle equipped with courage, skill, strength, endurance, love and fortitude. These impressions are the little points of illumination and are simultaneously of considerable satisfaction in a dark world of violence and tragedy.[36]

Other Indian academic critics and general readers believe that the core of *A Farewell to Arms* is found in its very powerful dramatization of liberal humanism. S. S. Sangwan and Satyapal Dahiya, for instance, disagree with Western critics who view that the novel is written in the tradition of naturalism. They contend that Western critics are off the mark because they have not properly discussed the nature of artistic vision in Hemingway. Sangwan and Dahiya go on to say that

> the vision affirmed through the novel is rooted in Hemingway's personality, but that does not mean that anything or everything that Hemingway did or said in his life is either relevant to or important for a study of the integrated set of values which finds expression in this work.[37]

They take exception with those Western critics who view the novel as an example of Hemingway's pessimistic and even nihilistic view of life, or read the novel as an affirmation of stoic dignity, or as a dramatization of the Christian mode of salvation: "None of the [Western] critics who discuss Hemingway's artistic vision have been able to reach the heart of the novel which, it seems, lies in its very powerful dramatization of the central principles of liberal humanism."[38]

According to Sangwan and Dahiya, the principles of liberal humanism are the real center of strength of *A Farewell to Arms*; and if the principles of liberal humanism are its real strength, then Fredric Henry is indeed their standard bearer. They develop their argument as follows:

> Fredric Henry represents the principles of liberal humanism quite convincingly in the novel. The war-experience does come as a great blow to him and the shattering experience makes him prone to skepticism bordering on cynicism. But he does not live and act in a state of moral vacuum for long and his humanism does assert itself soon, albeit in an attenuated form. He had come to the battlefront to serve humanity. He was inspired by his humanistic fervor to face hazards and dangers of war even in lands that are hundreds of miles away from his home. And his commitment to humanity does not break down under the severest test. The way he drives the ambulance and brings chocolate for his fellow beings under bombardment provides evidence of his devotion to something beyond his biological self. At the dressing station he insists on accepting medical aid only after those who are wounded more seriously have been attended to. Even when wounded he does not want to go back to his home. He has come as a volunteer and chooses to go again to the battlefront after his recovery from the wound. This is evidence of a firm devotion to the principle of human service even at the risk of his own life and comforts. As a liberal humanist, virtue for him lies in acting in accordance with the best impulses which exist in every individual, and which embrace all humanity in fellowship. He does his duties not out of obedience to some authority outside him but out of an inner devotion to the cause. His humanistic commitment enables him to enter into meaningful relationships with others. He is fighting to protect certain ways and values of life. And in this he relies only upon his human potentialities, his own inner strength and not upon any external or transcendent source like Christianity or books like the *Black Pig*. Fredric Henry overcomes his ego and identifies himself with his struggling fellow beings and through his devotion to these ideas tries to make his life purposive and meaningful.[39]

Next, Fredric Henry moves on to further his growth and self-fulfillment to brave the challenges of life that lie ahead of him. Thus, Sangwan and Dahiya find that

> *A Farewell to Arms* is a record of how the protagonist responds to challenges in life in his onward march to self-realization. The inexorable and ruthless process of the logic of human life forces him to fall back upon his personal sources for strength. It is only through his unflinching devotion to the sanctity of human personality and a

reverence for human life and freedom that he can muster sufficient strength to face difficult challenges. Impelled by his humanistic impulses, he even goes to the extent of revolting against mechanical and inhuman discipline of the military world.[40]

In addition, Sangwan and Dahiya find further evidence that Fredric Henry is a liberal humanist in his attitude toward love, not just war:

> As in war, so in love, Henry's behavior is illustrative of Hemingway's commitment to humanism. Love for Rinaldi, a cynical skeptic, is a mere sexual orgy which is over in just half an hour or fifteen minutes. It overwhelms him with disgust and despair but Henry, like a true humanist, brings to his sexual life with Catherine the finer human feelings of companionship, sympathy and mutual regard. The love, which began as a casual sexual affair, grows into a mature and passionate love based upon the involvement of their full personalities. It leads both of them to mutual fulfillment. Their love enables Henry to wash out the bad taste of his encounter with the carabinieres. They make a home which gives them peace and delight. It may be mentioned here in passing that the humanism, which is being affirmed through Henry, is not as bold and comprehensive as it should be at its best. The tradition of liberal humanism to which Hemingway belongs went into a defensive posture in the twentieth century. The only viable course to protect one's freedom and self-respect is seen now in a strategic withdrawal, which leaves scope for selective involvement with others through personal relationships alone.[41]

Moreover, Sangwan and Dahiya find that Hemingway's attitude toward success in life as depicted through the character of Frederic Henry also "shows his identification with the liberal humanist tradition:"

> The view of success based upon wealth and social reputation clashes violently with Hemingway's view of man's happiness and fulfillment. The writer treats Count Greffi in a sarcastically ironic manner for his pride in playing billiards so well. His notion of success in terms of playing a game well or living for a hundred years is in sharp contrast with Henry's notion of success, which is based upon commitment to some noble human cause and living a life of purposive action and integrity. Henry's humanistic code of values does not admit any element of careerism or self-aggrandizement.[42]

Thus, in *A Farewell to Arms*, Hemingway established his own brand of liberal humanism through the actions, behavior, and examples set by Fredric Henry. Decidedly, for some Indian critics such as Sangwan and Dahiya, Hemingway's novel is an extension of the "creative powers of this philosophy."[43]

Adding to the range and complexity of critical views of *A Farewell to Arms*, Aparajita Nanda finds that *A Farewell to Arms*, among other works by Hemingway, reflects the author's search for identity and a preoccupation with the notion of androgyny and its concomitant homosexuality and lesbianism, which Nanda refers to as "his desire as a perversion."[44] Nanda writes that

> in Hemingway, the male-female pseudo-twinning, I feel, left its mark. He grew up with a sense of insecurity about his gender, and often in private life as well as in his writings manifested a preoccupation with gender-crossing, which expressed itself in his fondness for short-haired women. Short-haired women carried in themselves the ambiguity of feminine identity—the short hair indicating their maleness. Hemingway's fascination with short-haired women obviously had androgynous reverberations. And so repeatedly in his novels there is a predominant feeling of sexual ambivalence. And yet, the very impulse, which pulled Hemingway towards androgyny, also made him feel a sense of shame and anger. This led him to try and (sic) dismiss his desire as a perversion and rise above it.[45]

Citing the characters of the nurses in *A Farewell to Arms*, Nanda feels that "Hemingway's preoccupation with androgyny entailed . . . a look at homosexuality and lesbianism:"[46]

> In *A Farewell to Arms* nurse Ferguson's attitude towards Catherine is not only protective but also domineering. She slices through Catherine and Henry's illusions of getting married, writing it off as 'You'll never get married. . . . You'll fight before you'll marry. . . . You'll die then. Fight or die. That's what people do. They don't marry.' Her bitterness takes on an added meaning when she rebuffs Henry and declares in an ominous tone 'But watch out you don't get her in trouble. You get her in trouble and I'll kill you.' Her warning speaks of more than mere concern for a friend. Later on when Henry comes back from the front and finds Fergie and Catherine in a hotel, there is an obvious possessiveness in her speech. Jealousy is written large all over and the lesbian undertone is quickly overwritten by repeated mentions of prudish morality.[47]

Finally, arguing that "It was probably easier for Hemingway to deal with love between the same sexes rather than create an androgynous being,"[48] Nanda speculates that Hemingway's "dilemma of gender contributed to the turmoil which finally pushed the writer towards suicide."[49]

Insofar as Hemingway's fictional characters are realistic and autobiographical, Nanda's analysis provides insights into his characters and their relationships that were not previously considered. Yet to the extent that Nanda's view of Hemingway's novels is based on a notion of gender confusion and a kind of innuendo in which characters are seen as fixed personalities irrespective of the forces acting upon them, Hemingway's "dilemma of gender" is limited in accounting for the popularity of Hemingway's works. Nanda's view seems to suggest that his popularity speaks to—or can be reduced to—a similar "desire as perversion" among his readers, irrespective of the historical contexts and themes of his novels and the psychological development of his characters over the course of the action. Most readers of Hemingway would find this notion surprising, if not aesthetically simplistic.

When all is said and done, Indian critics and general readers alike come to a consensus that Hemingway's *A Farewell to Arms* is one of the world's greatest novels dealing with love on a human level and politics on an international level—with an anti-war slant—a philosophy cherished by the vast multitude of the Indian population. For the patricians as well as the plebeians in India, love reigns supreme and war is, indeed, hell! In this genre, Hemingway could not be appreciated more.

Courage to Resist

Many Indian academic critics as well as general readers consider *For Whom the Bell Tolls* as Hemingway's finest as well his most popular novel. They agree on the general meaning of the novel as a story of courageous resistance to tyranny, and that this resistance is felt as a concern for all humanity. As Dr. Ramesh Srivastava of the English department at Guru Nanak Dev University in Amritsar writes,

> With the help of synecdoche, Hemingway has raised this episode of the three-day bridge-blowing operation into a universal theme of the brotherhood of man where human beings are interrelated by their mutual concern and at the same time maintain their individuality. . . . If the bell tolls for Jordan, it tolls for the rest of humanity.[50]

The protagonist Robert Jordan is "involved in mankind," not as a Marxist, but as a believer in "Liberty, Equality, and Fraternity." This novel not only tells the story of a single small action during the Spanish Civil War, that is, the blowing up of a bridge at the precise time when Fascist reinforcements must be halted, but also the story of the guerillas with whom Robert Jordan must work, and his love for Maria, a refuge girl, which must be fulfilled within three days of his mission. According to Ramji Lall,

> of all of Hemingway's stories, this is the richest in individual, convincing characters. . . . And the action of the story, while not more vivid or more swiftly paced than that of other Hemingway novels, is realized with a unique adequacy and fullness. Although *For Whom the Bell Tolls* does not wholly escape the usual limitations of Hemingway, it is his one novel which, in sheer massiveness, in the detailed and living portrayal of an entire area of life, belongs with such earlier American fiction as Theodore Dreiser's *The Financier* or Willa Cather's *My Antonia*.[51]

Lall finds that the character of Robert Jordan differs from Fredric Henry only in Jordan's recognition of the meaning of the sermon of poet John Donne quoted at the start of the novel: "No man is an island, entire of itself." Yet this character marks a development:

> The critics who saw in this book merely a tract for the Loyalist cause in the Spanish Civil War were not reading Hemingway. For him now there were two parties to every alienation: the man and his society. His canvas was larger, his theme the same. Jordan fights for the Loyalist cause, but his is a private war. He is forever at odds with the Spanish guerillas with whom he hides out in the mountain cave while waiting for the moment to come when he may blow up his bridge and so fulfill his destiny. Political theories and programs have little to do with the motives of Pilar, the earth woman, who commands her weakling mate Pablo; and it is in the intense and physical love for a woman of his kind rather than in self-sacrifice for a cause that Jordan finds his reasons for life and for death. The stupidity and suspicions of both parties to the political conflict cancel out any immediate social significance to Jordan's sacrifice. He loves Maria, he blows up the bridge, he meets a meaningless death in fight; but he has heard the bell toll.[52]

Thus, Jordan can die with a sense of accomplishment.

The title suggests that because death is inevitable, the importance of a man lies in how he can best make use of his life before he embraces death. According to Srivastava,

> Thus though the end of the book is tragic, it cannot be called pessimistic. Robert Jordan lies on the pine needled floor, waiting for his death, but he has made the best use of his life. He has fought for a cause in which he believed, is educated in the process of helping others, and brings a message at the end that the world is a good place for living and is worth fighting for. . . . It may be concluded that Hemingway, who had struggled all his life and particularly in the Spanish Civil War, had realized that a man cannot struggle alone against gigantic odds, that he is part of humanity, and that failures should not discourage him from his struggle for great achievements.[53]

To express implicit meanings in his stories and novels, Hemingway often applied the "iceberg principle" in his writing. In *Death in the Afternoon*, Hemingway writes, "The dignity of movement of an ice-berg is due to only one-eighth of it being above water."[54] This metaphorical iceberg epitomizes Hemingway's writing style and his narrative capabilities as the art of "understatement." According to Srivastava,

> The difference between an artist and amateur is that whereas the former uses his medium of art with subtlety and achieves the maximum effect with a few master touches, the latter consciously strives to achieve perfection by using every conceivable device—symbolism, allegory, imagery, figures of speech—like Indian brides who mar their natural beauty by wearing gaudy colored dresses and

glittering ornaments—on head, in nose, in ears, in neck, in hands, in feet, and almost at every conceivable place, and become no more than mere walking showcases of ornaments. The most appropriate technique in any form of art is the subtle use of a few devices to enhance the natural beauty and to imbue it with meanings without the impression of artificiality.[55]

Hemingway uses two literary devices—symbolism and irony—to suggest his larger meanings. Symbolism and irony have many things in common: they carry more than their surface meanings, are indirect and sophisticated in nature, appeal to the intelligence of the reader, and can be found in words, events, and situations. But whereas symbolism carries an implied likeness, irony emphasizes disparity. In *For Whom the Bell Tolls*, Srivastava writes that "For Hemingway who believed in understatements and in achieving maximum effect by using a minimum of words, both symbolism and irony were suitable."[56]

First, with regard to symbolism, Srivastava notes that

> *For Whom the Bell Tolls*, in a rather loose sense, is a historical and political novel, since it is based on a small episode in the history of the Spanish Civil War. Any such work of art ceases to be significant to future generations unless it is imbued with the deep meanings and truths of life. With the use of symbols, Hemingway has transformed the novel about the Spanish Civil War into a parable of the artist and his survival in a fascist world, and of the virgin Spanish earth being exploited and ravaged by the cruel industrial and war machines. The tragedy of the bridge becomes the tragedy of the Spanish earth and its people.[57]

On another level, the Civil War is a struggle of the people who want to protect and sustain their traditional pristine ways of life, much simpler and much closer to nature, against the highly mechanized and destructive Fascist society. Pilar and Robert Jordan are their only hope. According to Srivastava,

> Pilar symbolizes the Spanish character itself, a mixture of the tough and the tender—tough for leadership and fighting, tender for parental concern, love and care. Like other Spanish people, she is superstitious, thinks of her own past, and is concerned with the Republic. . . . The Fascists with their tanks and airpower symbolize doom to the Spanish people. . . . The bridge symbolizes not only the fate of the Republic but also an object to be secured and utilized by the Spanish guerillas.[58]

Employing natural symbols to convey the ultimate fate of those who struggle, Hemingway uses the mountains as a symbol. According to Srivastava, "It is in the mountains that El Sordo's and Pablo's bands are destroyed. It is also in the mountains that Jordan waits for his death."[59]

In the last chapter of *For Whom the Bell Tolls*, Robert Jordan is lying on the pine trunks waiting for the attack to resume so that he can blow up the bridge.

He tries to calm his fear and notices a squirrel. Srivastava relates this episode to the story of an Indian king, explaining, "Here Hemingway uses the 'objective epitome' technique to explain the subjective conditions of Jordan:"[60]

> An Indian king, having been defeated several times by his enemy, saw a spider taking its prey on a smooth marble wall from which it fell unsuccessfully on the floor many times. Not only did the king find his own subjective conditions objectified there, but when the spider did succeed, he saw it an epitome of universal struggle and success. The squirrel and the spider are simply agents for externalizing the emotions of Jordan and the Indian king. These characters also release the tension in their minds by identifying themselves with these creatures.[61]

Srivastava summarizes Hemingway's use of symbols to allude to the layers of meaning in his novels, as follows:

> One great achievement of Hemingway's art is that by means of his narrative skill, he creates his characters in such a way that they can stand on many symbolic levels. He achieves this by making them simple, unadorned in superfluous details, and equipped with reflective qualities by which they assume different shapes and colors from the reader's mind. Sometimes even one of their traits or incidents of life becomes a significant symbol; thus, Jake Barnes' wound stands for the sterility and frustration of the generation of the 1920s, Catherine Barkley for domesticity and home-life, and Santiago's fight with the sharks for the struggle of humanity against hostile elements of nature. In *For Whom the Bell Tolls*, the raping of Maria can stand for the exploitation of poor, defenseless people, the destruction of peace and happiness of domestic life which she represents, the inhumanity of man against man, and the ravaging of the virgin, primitive Spanish earth by the devastating machines.[62]

The second literary device that Hemingway uses throughout *To Whom the Bell Tolls* is irony, beginning with the title. At the end of his narrative, what is usually taken to be an optimistic concluding statement is full of irony: "I have fought for what I believed in for a year now. If we win here we will win everywhere. The world is a fine place and worth the fighting for and I hate very much to leave it. . . . I wish there was some way to pass on what I've learned though. Christ I was learning fast there at the end."[63] Srivastava explains the use of irony in this statement as follows:

> We know that Robert Jordan fought not so much for the Loyalists as he did against the Fascists. Even his blowing up of the bridge was largely due to Golz's orders, which he considered defective. The hope of winning everywhere depends on winning here and Robert Jordan knows that the defeat is imminent. He also knows how fine the Spanish part of the world is, in which mutual killings and atrocities are everyday occurrences. And what he had learned about

the Spanish people was not all very pleasant.[64]

Throughout the work, the use of irony of the situation conveys the tension between hope and despair:

> The Spanish Civil War in *For Whom the Bell Tolls* provides an ironical situation in that the Loyalists and Fascists fight against each other and destroy Spain in the name of saving it and its values. The former accuses the latter of inhuman atrocities and massacres while they themselves are no less guilty. . . . Robert Jordan, who said that he has no time for girls, finds that in the three-day period, Maria and his desire to live become almost as much the matter of his concern as the blowing up of the bridge. Pablo, leader of a Loyalist guerilla band, steals the detonator and hinders the blowing of the bridge while he is expected to do otherwise. Augustin, a guerilla on guard, demands the second half of the password from Robert Jordan, while he himself does not know the first half. Rafael, the gypsy, in place of noting the movement of military vehicles, goes to shoot rabbits.[65]

Thus, Indian critics appreciate Hemingway's uses of both symbolism and irony in telling the story in *For Whom the Bell Tolls*:

> While serving his artistic purpose, they [symbolism and irony] do not interfere with the story of the novel. There are places where the story, its symbolism, and its irony—like the Ganges, the Jamuna, and the Saraswati—merge together to form the Sangam of deep meanings and metaphysical implications. . . . Like three foreigners calling an object by three different names, many symbolists, ironists and realists claim Hemingway under their own brand names, not knowing that he belongs to all of them.[66]

At the same time, Indian academic critics and general readers appreciate *For Whom the Bell Tolls* as a Spanish tragedy:

> Any interpretation of *For Whom the Bell Tolls* is bound to be incomplete without considering it as a great tragedy. For not only has it two of the main elements—great action and great character, but also soliloquies of the hero, the observation of the unities of time and place which make it a thoroughly Aristotelian tragedy. It is a tragedy, too, in the sense of depicting an unfortunate period in the life of a nation when Robert Jordan, representing the Loyalist forces in Spain, is wounded fatally in his symbolic fight against the villainous forces of the Fascist Government.[67]

Noting that "the basis of tragedy is an action, a sequence of events in time related to an object, or complex of objects, which is capable of being perceived as a termination of that particular sequence," T. R. Henn points out that "the problem of the tragic playwright would appear to be to refract, condense, and reorganize that experience."[68] Accordingly, Henn argues that the artist must have a free hand to reorganizes and handle the raw material of tragedy. In the case of *For Whom the Bell Tolls*, Hemingway has created a miniature of the Spanish Civil War, whose layers of tragedy culminate in one man's mission and the events and lives of a handful of people over a three-day period:

> In *For Whom the Bell Tolls*, Hemingway dramatizes historic, political and social conditions of the Spanish Civil War synecdochically by depicting Jordan's task of blowing up the bridge with the help of guerrillas to facilitate the Loyalist offensive. In itself, the entire action of the novel is confined to three days and involves a handful of people including a few guerillas working for Jordan, but in order to make the ordinary extraordinary, to build up the tragic momentum appropriate for the theme, to bring the past in alignment with the present, to enlist the sympathy of the reader by preparing him for 'willing suspension of disbelief' and to develop characters from various angles by giving a certain length to the plot, Hemingway has drawn into it the whole of the Spanish Civil War with its components of love, violence and death, on a small canvas. The plot, as such, is not only sufficiently long, and has depth, but with the help of sub-plots, symbolism, rhythm and imagery produces the impression of a complete and complex action. All dreadful elements of the Civil War, which horrified the Spanish people between July 1936 and March 1939, have been depicted on a reduced scale. In place of an army, we have about a dozen guerillas. A few machine guns and rifles replace tanks and airplanes. The blowing up of the bridge is like conquering a kingdom. Small incidents of indiscipline and betrayal, cruelty and torture epitomize countless cases of deception, destruction, rape and massacre, which took place on both sides in the Civil War. The action of blowing up the bridge and the consequent fatal wound of Jordan become the tragedy of the Spanish Civil War in microcosm.[69]

According to Aristotle, "Of simple plots and actions, the episodic are the worst." Aristotle goes on to define "episodic plot" as one "in which the episodes are not arranged according to the law of probability and necessity."[70] The Indian critic Srivastava would disagree with the view that Hemingway's compression of the Spanish Civil War into a three-day bridge-blowing action lacks in originality and that the novel is a mere showpiece in its depiction of humanity. On the contrary, "Far from limiting his view by telescoping time and action, Hemingway has shown an intensity of action and depth and has successfully raised the action of blowing up the bridge to a universal level."[71] Srivastava also disagrees with Lionel Trilling's assertion that this novel is an "astonishing melodrama" in which the hero has acted in a cinematic story without exemplifying "the moral and political tension which existed in the historical situation,"[72] finding it far from accurate:

> To confine Hemingway's novel within the limits of political and historical situations as they prevailed at the time of the Spanish Civil War would be to narrow down the meaning and scope of the action.

A great novelist, besides being aware of what happens around him, must adequately portray the political and moral tensions without restricting himself to them. Instead, he must raise them to a universal level. Robert Jordan is concerned not only with the moral and political tensions of Spain as such but also with the whole of humanity.[73]

Moreover, like Dante's great poem which deals with love, war and death, *For Whom the Bell Tolls* encompasses all three subjects.

In Shakespeare's plays, the tragic sense is usually, though not always, achieved in the hero's fall from nobility or higher stature. Hemingway's tragic heroes are more complex. Srivastava finds that "Hemingway's heroes are simple men, ennobled by their honor, courage and perseverance. The tragic sense in his works comes when the hero, who, in spite of his attained nobility, gets wounded, dies or fails to achieve his goals due to his tragic flaws or failures."[74] Like Aristotle's classical Western hero, he is "the man of much glory and good fortune who is not [too] superior in excellence and uprightness and yet does not come into his misfortune because of baseness and rascality but through some inadequacy or positive fault."[75] According to Srivastava,

> In Hemingway's heroes the frailty lays not so much in an inadequate knowledge or the error of judgment as in the underestimation of their circumstances and overconfidence in their capabilities. From one angle, this could be considered a defect of character, which causes sufferings. The heroes have power and capability but fail in the execution of their aims largely because they ignore or underestimate the warnings of danger particularly in relation to the limitations of their own capabilities. In *The Old Man and the Sea*, Santiago is tempted to an excess of power beyond his capacity—an act of hubris—not only by considering himself a great fisherman and by going "too far out" alone in the sea but by fighting with inadequate arms against sharks. Jordan is a man of action—determined and courageous, but also at times nervous and hesitant. He is not fully conscious of his flaw, the residue of which makes him defenseless at many points.[76]

For example, Jordan's weakness for Maria makes him break the rule of leaving women alone, thus temporarily diluting his resolve when his desire to live overpowers his will to act firmly and to face death fearlessly. This desire to live is at the heart of Hemingway's sense of tragedy:

> So far she had not affected his resolution but he would much prefer not to die. He would abandon a hero's or a martyr's end gladly. He did not want to make a Thermopylae, nor be a Horatius at any bridge, nor be the Dutch boy with his finger in that dyke. No. He would like to spend some time with Maria. That was the simplest expression of it. He would like to spend a long, long time with her.[77]

The tension between this desire to live and the will to face death fearlessly is ongoing and invokes the reader's identification with the tragic hero until the end:

> Throughout *For Whom the Bell Tolls* the hero is beset with all these: obstacles, dangers, forebodings, forewarnings, and weaknesses; thus he gets the premonition of an inevitable catastrophe. All these symptoms also serve another dramatic function: They create suspense and accordingly raise the interest of the Indian readers. First-time Indian readers of the novel repeatedly ask: "Is Robert Jordan going to succeed in his mission?" Of course, they expect to see Jordan succeed. And this expectation of the readers coupled with Jordan's high-risk mission create suspense in the novel.[78]

Up until the final moments, readers wait anxiously for Jordan to finish the mining of the bridge, for they apprehend that it might not be completed, and that Jordan might die in the process without completing his mission:

> The building up of suspense brings an anticipated end to the novel with its hero waiting for his death. For the supreme misfortune to which the hero comes through his error or frailty—in Jordan's case by overconfidence or trust misplaced—is terminated with death and so with it the tragic as well as aesthetic experience. The lifetime experiences of the hero crystallize at the time of his death into an essence by which the author affirms new values, by recalling his heroic deeds. The curtain is drawn at the height of the emotional pitch. The conflict is resolved.[79]

As Jordan looks down the mountain slopes, he affirms the humanity of his struggle and embraces the ultimate irony of death because of how he has lived in his final days. The hero has been transformed by his ultimate task:

> I have fought for what I believed in for a year now. If we win here we will win everywhere. The world is a fine place and worth the fighting for and I hate very much to leave it. And you had a lot of luck, he told himself, to have had such a good life. You've had just as good a life as grandfather's though not as long. You've had as good a life as any one because of these last days. You do not want to complain when you have been so lucky.[80]

Thus, the reader can accept the fate of the tragic hero without sentimentality. The humanity of the three days becomes the lesson of a lifetime.

Defiance as Heroism

Of all of the Hemingway novels, *The Old Man and the Sea* is the most popular to both the Indian academic critics as well as to the general readers. Since the publication of *The Old Man and the Sea* in 1953, both young and old alike have read the book more than once and have visited the theaters to watch the movie version with Spencer Tracy as old man Santiago. For these people, the interest in the novel as well as in the movie has remained unabated. For Hemingway to be read, loved, appreciated and admired by millions of ordinary Indians from a non-western culture—for one book alone if not for more—is a tremendous feat by the author. If Hemingway's writing style accounts for fifty percent of the novel's popularity, the other fifty percent comes from his unique creation of the character of Santiago and his concomitant calling of fishing. Indeed, the class of fishermen in India find in Santiago their own double as well as their daily predicament that their calling brings forth. When out on the sea or on the river, as part of their struggle for livelihood, these Indian fishermen know that Santiago is with them, at least in spirit, that he becomes their St. James the Lesser.

Indian academic critics, however, look at *The Old Man and the Sea* from different points of view. As Dr. S. C. Mundra of the English department at Bareilly College writes,

> It is a naturalistic novel with a humanistic outcome, a tale of ritual encounter between the old Cuban fisherman and the forces of erosion itself, as he battles first with a giant marlin, which he tames and catches, then with the predatory sharks that reduce the prize to a skeleton he nevertheless brings home to port. The mode is simple and epical, a method of symbolic allegory with powerful Christian allusions; its lesson seems far away from Hemingway's early note of nihilism, but was implicit in . . . its myth of heroism, humility, and the moral virtues of endurance.[81]

According to Dr. Sobha Chattopadhyay, professor of Comparative Literature at Jadavpur University in Kolkata, *The Old Man and Sea* stands apart from Hemingway's previous novels:

> *The Old Man and the Sea* is different from the other previous novels—the adventure stories with brilliant surface texture, combining realism and mythical elements. This little novel is a parable of man's power to endure what appears to be the inexorable ways of an impersonal Nature. Of course the theme of tight-lipped suffering links it with the earlier novels. Santiago is representative of suffering humanity; one cannot but admire the qualities he gains from his loss, that is, heroism, humility, and a sense of brotherhood with his fellow creatures.[82]

Overall Indian scholars regard *The Old Man and the Sea* from a number of points of view such as realism, existentialism, symbolism, elements of sainthood, elements of martyrdom, psychology of heroic living, and code hero. Indian scholars who view the novel as a realistic piece of writing note two levels of reality in the novels of Hemingway. The first level is external or objective reality. In its broadest sense, external or objective reality in *The Sun Also Rises*, *A Farewell to Arms* and *For Whom the Bell Tolls* stands for the impersonal war environment and its associated factors such as death, disaster and other relevant circumstances. However, in *The Old Man and the Sea*, Sanjukta Dasgupta finds that

> the external or objective reality represents not the war background of the previous novels but the indifferent natural environment, especially the sea. The war background and the natural background are similar in the sense that both are hostile to isolated human excellence.[83]

The second level of reality is subjective reality, representing the perceptional world of the human mind in an interaction with objective reality. Thus, the two worlds represented by the two levels of reality—that is, the external world and the world of the individual ego—are seen to be in constant interaction in Hemingway's novels, thereby lending his texts considerable dynamism. According to Dasgupta,

> In *The Old Man and the Sea* the two levels of reality in Hemingway's novels—subjective and objective—that is, Santiago's inner world of private pride, grief, expectation and self-awareness and the external world of the natural phenomena meet at a point, when Santiago senses that he is after all a part of the universe.[84]

Although Hemingway is not classified as an existentialist, he has dealt with many of its major themes. As Alladi observes,

> Santiago, in *The Old Man and the Sea* is alienated from his people because he had been unlucky for eighty-four days. He is aware of the absurdity of man's existence. The old man's nausea is a representation of the absurd—of man pitted against the enormous universe. His triumph at capturing the marlin is questioned by the attacking sharks. However, he does not give up his struggle; instead fights against defeat insisting that 'A man can be destroyed but not defeated.'[85]

But Alladi also finds Santiago is an authentic individual who is aware of the importance of the present. Quoting from the novel, Alladi explains,

> 'The thousand times that he had proved it meant nothing. Now he was proving it again. Each time was a new time and he never thought about the past when he was doing it.' He had been an ace fisherman in his youth but he wants to become one again. For him, becoming thus is very important. He makes the vital decision of venturing deep into the sea 'to go there to find him beyond all people.' And when he is attacked by the sharks, he takes full responsibility of the situation and does not accept defeat. He is not a conventional believer, though

he repeats 'ten Our Fathers and ten Hail Marys.' But he believes in the full potential of man: 'I will show him [the marlin] what a man can do and what a man endures.' He decides to fight against all odds until his death: '"Fish," he said softly, aloud, "I'll stay with you until I am dead."'[86]

Some Indian academic critics discern symbolism in *The Old Man and the Sea*, noting parallels among Herman Melville's *Moby Dick*, Joseph Conrad's *Lord Jim*, and Hemingway's *The Old Man and the Sea*. According to Murari Prasad, reader in English at D. S. College in Katihar, Bihar, in all three novels,

> the massive watery locale is an inalienable part of the fictional world. . . . The sea becomes a capacious symbol not only to carry the narrative spine but also the thematic burden. . . . The sea is a symbol surrounded by secondary symbols like ship, voyage, whale, sailing, fishing, the marlin and sharks; it captures the gap between the sentient and the insentient non-self, man and nature, the man-acting and the combative, war-like, conflict-ridden complex world.[87]

But Prasad finds a different use of the sea in *The Old Man and the Sea*, noting that,

> the seascape in Hemingway's story becomes the operative alternative reality on which man can impose order, exercise his will, and attain selfhood through his exertion and strenuous work. Voyage is very important in *Moby Dick*, whereas sailing and fishing constitute the key action in *Lord Jim* and *The Old Man and the Sea*, respectively.[88]

In *Moby Dick*, Ahab realizes that the sea is ambiguously both redemption and death; it is divine but always inhuman. According to Prasad, Santiago also experiences this duality in *The Old Man and the Sea*:

> The seascape with its primitive lineaments offers Santiago the ritual of life and death. In describing Santiago's vital relationship to the sea, Hemingway underlines man's primal urge to stay in touch with first things and to test his very being against its limits. The sea as the source of both sustenance and annihilation tests Santiago to the limits of his endurance. In its varying moods, it is merciful and minatory, bountiful and unconcerned, life-supporting and deceitful. In its inscrutable and erratic ways, it resembles creation, which gives and takes away its gifts without logic and reason. It contains both the marlin and sharks, and the grand cycle of life and death is seen in its bosom and wavy swell.[89]

Thus, Prasad notes that the sea is a "common symbol" essential to all three novels:

> The essential themes of the three novels, although impressive contrasts, are wedded to the sea. In *Moby Dick*, it symbolizes the vast

cosmos, immensity and inscrutability of nature in which Ahab launches the voyage to sight the ultimate truth. In Conrad's book, it provides the background for the crisis or the test of the shipman, and in Hemingway's *The Old Man and the Sea* it replicates the combative world with little leeway for soft options. As regards man's place in this world and his limited capacity for defining his existential autonomy, these writers share the same angle of vision. And the sea—their common symbol—adds overpluses of meaning to this vision by giving additional body to the narrative and insinuating hidden layers of suggestion for the symbiosis of this vision.[90]

Because of Santiago's Christian virtues, humility, piety, compassion, morality and simplicity, many Indian critics describe him as saintly, if not "a saint of the sea" in a real sense. As Tripathi notes, "In *The Old Man and the Sea*, [Hemingway] tries to depict an ideal, old, simple and primitive man who comes very close to becoming a saint."[91] Santiago's sainthood is manifested in his compassion even when he has to kill the fish for sustenance. Nair concurs, finding that,

> in a world where everything kills everything else, it celebrates man's regulated self-aggression and his powers of endurance. Santiago's personal struggle involves both internal violence and a worldly struggle inevitably tied up with failure. The old man with this vast experience and supreme skill, in the fight with the strange marlin far out in the sea, practices compassionate violence. He ruminates on the right of the fish to fight, to assert his strength, even though he is confident that the ultimate triumph will be his.[92]

Some Indian academic critics find a modernist quest for martyrdom in *The Old Man and the Sea* by Hemingway's use of Jesus as a symbol and image of divinity in man or as the image of man merging into divinity. Hemingway invokes the divine quality of Jesus in the character of Santiago. As Subhas Sarkar, former head and Shakespeare professor of English at Rabindra Bharati University in Kolkata, notes,

> Jesus bearing his own Cross and then nailed to the Cross and suffering till he realizes God's grace, are the recurring ideas of martyrdom which Hemingway presents through a number of his protagonists, especially Santiago in *The Old Man and the Sea*.[93]

Referring to the definitions of *martyr* given in the *Shorter Oxford English Dictionary* as "one who undergoes death (or great suffering) on behalf of any belief or cause or through devotion to some object" or as "one who voluntarily undergoes the penalty of death for refusing to renounce the Christian faith or for obedience to any law or command of the Church," Sarkar writes,

> We have illustrations of these two different types of martyr in Hemingway's *The Old Man and the Sea* . . . with the added

implication of the celebration of the ritual act of the greatest Christian martyr, Jesus, who went through successive stages of Hubris or pride, sin (out of ignorance of the will and design of God), purification through perfection of will and suffering which is largely passive in nature, and endurance and final submission.[94]

Santiago's personality evolves gradually into the role of a martyr after Santiago has been declared by his fellow fishermen as *salao* (the worst form of unlucky) for having failed to catch a fish for eight-four days, and he goes out alone in his skiff in the Gulf Stream, where it swings in above the long island of Cuba. He maintains his pride in going out all alone (when Manolin, the young boy whom he had taught the art of fishing was dissuaded by his parents from accompanying him and to switch over to others' boats) far beyond the range of other fishermen. At the same time, Hemingway writes, "He has his simplicity and honesty to realize at the end that he has transgressed the limits."[95]

According to Sarkar, "By attaining this humility, he arrives at the proper understanding of the true meaning of suffering."[96] Besides humility, Santiago has natural piety and compassion:

> What really impresses pursuit of a quest—quest for martyrdom, is to achieve his self-realization through initial pride (violating his own luck), consequent sin (killing of the impressive-looking marlin whom he calls a brother), relentless suffering and compassion. But in his sense of endurance there is an assertion of the idea of man's ceaseless struggle for survival.[97]

According to Sarkar, Santiago achieves victory over defeat when he takes his stand like a military commander who vows to fight to the last to hold his line against overwhelming enemy superiority:

> Here Santiago is a martyr for human struggle for survival. Though not outwardly religious, Santiago believes that in killing the giant-size marlin, he has committed a sin, but then he justifies himself by arguing that later by loving it he came to (sic) overcome his sin and says that he had killed it for survival, as all men do. He also attains the final humility when he understands that he had (sic) gone beyond the limits and hence, paid the price for it: 'I went out too far' He has also prayed several times for divine interception in his favor while battling with a wicked pack of jaws, although he has retained his unflinching faith in himself. 'Fight them,' he said. 'I'll fight them until I die.' This mixture of self-confidence (which also speaks of a sense of pride), compassion and courage, suffering and heroic resistance, followed by a sense of humility marks him out as a martyr.[98]

However, although Santiago believes he has committed a sin and he prays for divine interception, he is not a martyr in a Christian sense:

He is not a Christian martyr like Becket in Eliot's *Murder in The Cathedral* but a martyr for a human cause—his own survival, no less religious in his commitment to the cause than Becket himself. When he reaches the shore with his harpoon and the oar lost in the sea and the marlin reduced to a skeleton, himself physically battered and weakened, yet undefeated in his struggle against the odds at sea, for sheer survival, he is like Jesus on the Cross in the final moment of his glory.[99]

His cause is a human cause and his humanity is undefeated: this is the measure of a man, not a saint. In words best left to Hemingway, "But man is not made for defeat," he said. "A man can be destroyed but not defeated."[100]

Although Indian academic critics such as Sarkar brand Santiago as a non-Christian martyr, others discount the presence of Christian symbolism and crucifixion analogy in the novel. Instead, they find the psychology of heroic living in Santiago much more evident and important. As Satyanarain Singh writes, "I think the crucifixion analogy burdens the novel with a meaning which cannot be sustained by its text. First, the old man is not dead and second, the forces which are responsible for Jesus' martyrdom are totally different from those affecting Santiago."[101]

According to A. H. Lass, Hemingway himself wanted his critics to follow this line of thought. As Hemingway wrote, "Sea equaled sea, old man was old man, the boy was a boy, the marlin was itself, and the Sharks were not better and not worse than other Sharks."[102] According to Hemingway, his task had been to convey Santiago's experience so exactly and directly that it became part of the reader's experience, freighted with all the implications that the reader could bring to it: "I tried to make a real old man, a real boy, a real sea, and a real fish and real sharks. But if I made them good and true enough they would mean many things."[103]

Singh downplays religious symbolism when he says, "Intellectual efforts to allegorize the narrative at each stage in religious or metaphysical terms not only give a false accent to Hemingway's thinking but also misrepresent the imaginative essence of the novel."[104] However, Singh tries to find a middle ground:

> The best acceptable position—if generalize we must—is to view the novel as a parable of human courage and valor in face of growing misfortunes and adversities. And what is of greater interest and importance is the study of the particular ways in which the old man thinks and acts under the growing pressure of circumstance, which like the octopus threatens to close on him from all directions.[105]

According to Singh, it is the old man's upright and uncompromising character against all odds that helps him achieve a heroic struggle, a struggle that distinguishes him from the rest of the mankind:

> He is an example of integral living wherein thought, emotion and

imagination always co-operate to strengthen and reinforce his will power in the fight against adversity—with hopes that ever remain paramount to his despairs. He would never allow his mind to get befogged by doubt or despair. His intellect works to clarify and decide and his will acts immediately on the decision with courage and determination. His loyalty to the profession—marked by humanity and compassion—builds up his power reserves. When in trouble, his imagination feeds on memory and lights up the incidents of valor and fortitude to cheer him up—or by an easy identification with the lovely objects around helps him imbibe strength through joy, and transcend his pain. Endowed with deep affection and aesthetic perception, Santiago has an extraordinary capacity for suffering, endurance and hope. Humble in success, courageous in failure, persevering in effort, confident in danger, practical in approach, clear in thought and prompt in action, the old man is the finest fruition of the heroic potentialities present in every man.[106]

In India, many people still view the Hemingway hero as a tough, hard-boiled brute who is obsessed by an appetite for bloody sports, drink, and women. But Santiago does not fulfill this image. As Lall writes,

> The Hemingway hero is, in fact, deeply sensitive, hard-bitten rather than hard-boiled, and suffering deeply from the painful effects of his experiences. It is only by being tough with himself that he can survive. It is perhaps by dealing in death that he can accept the fact of death.[107]

Philip Young, one of the first scholars to publish a book-length study on Hemingway, wrote that most of Hemingway's writings featured a "code hero" and a "Hemingway hero." As Lisa Tyler explains these terms, the Hemingway hero is the story's protagonist who has much to learn—and learns as the story progresses—about how to live in the world, while the code hero, who has the wisdom to know how to live properly, is—because of his adherence to an unspoken code of behavior—a mentor and example to the usually younger Hemingway hero.[108]

In *The Old Man and the Sea*, Manolin is the Hemingway hero learning how to live from Santiago, the code hero. In *A Farewell to Arms*, Frederic is the Hemingway hero who is learning the Hemingway code from Catherine, although, according to Lall, "The nearest approach to the code hero in this novel is the priest who tells Henry what is meant by true love and who finds comfort in his religious faith and in natural scenery."[109] Yet the code hero of *The Old Man and Sea* is unsurpassed:

> In *The Old Man and the Sea*, we see the code hero at his best. He is Santiago who brings us the message that, while a man may grow old and be wholly down on his luck, he can still dare to persist and win a victory by the very manner of his losing. After Santiago has caught a huge marlin, the sharks come and eat it up. But Santiago did catch the

marlin, he did fight well, he did all he could and it was a lot, and at the end he is happy. The great thing is not the victory but the struggle.[110]

Indeed, any fisherman in India can attest to this.

Conclusion

Across the divides of history, geography, and culture, the appreciation of literary works is often infused with meanings and nuances that reflect wider social, cultural and historical contexts not previously considered by an author's contemporaries or by readers and critics from an author's native land. The enthusiastic reception of Ernest Hemingway's short stories and novels by readers and scholars in Bangladesh and India after 1971 is remarkable in this regard. Although selected critical and scholarly works on Hemingway have been lost or are often hard to locate in Bangladesh and India, interviews with authoritative and representative readers, scholars and critics bear this out. Along with the available documentary sources, they corroborate the popularity of Hemingway across Bangladesh and India. Whether they read Hemingway in English or in translation, they avidly rediscover the humanity found in his works. Their commentaries are a tribute to Hemingway, the man and the legend.

Earlier Bangladeshi scholars and critics initially spoke of *The Sun Also Rises* and *A Farewell to Arms* as models of style for their exactitude, compactness, and preciseness; but *A Farewell to Arms* is the first book by Hemingway that struck a common chord among a great majority of people in Bangladesh in the aftermath of the civil war of 1971. Yet among all of Hemingway's works, *The Old Man and the Sea* receives their highest accolade. As a relatively new nation, Bangladeshis found in Santiago a postwar hero who was able to affirm life from scratch and give it a new meaning of dignity and pride. Only for a small number of Marxist critics does Santiago stand for the "poor and huddled masses" in Bangladesh.

Bangladeshis rank *The Old Man and the Sea* first among Hemingway's greatest achievements for its classic simplicity, its portrayal of the modern hero, and its moral endurance. Hasan Azizul Haque, one of the foremost short story writers of Bangladesh, admits reading time and again only one book: *The Old Man and the Sea*.[1]—Indeed, it is worth reading a thousand times.—*The Sun Also Rises* and *A Farewell to Arms* would be ranked second and third. *For Whom the Bell Tolls*, with its objectivity, epic proportions, and closely linked themes of love and death, would rank fourth. Bangladeshis favor these novels because, in one way or another, they explore themes that are relevant to their contemporary situations.

In prewar Bangladesh, Hemingway was already popular as the spokesman for the lost generation, as a great literary stylist, and—to the chagrin of the mullahs and Hindu priests—for his flamboyant lifestyle. Although he was an

American, his settings were usually foreign and therefore had a more universal appeal. Hemingway's style was also easy to read in translation, which is indicated by the popularity among ordinary readers of translations of his short stories.

Accordingly, one gathers that the reasons for Hemingway's popularity in Bangladesh, as a man and as an author, are manifold and complex. To find a comprehensive explanation would require investigations in sociology, cultural history, and national psychology as well as literature and literary criticism. Yet according to the first-hand accounts of his Bangladeshi readers, at least part of the explanation for the continued popularity of Hemingway in Bangladesh after 1971 is the overriding humanity entwined throughout his novels and short stories that speaks to their human condition, their struggles in life, and the fabric of their society. Whatever dilemmas they face, it is Hemingway's honesty and sincerity, his genuine concern for truth, and his unceasing and unconditional striving for his own artistic excellence that has won the admiration and respect of the Bangladeshi readers and the academic critics.

If Bangladeshis are generous in their recognition and reception of Hemingway as a constructive and lasting influence on Bengali literature, are general readers, scholars and critics in India far behind? Like Bangladeshis, Indian readers admire and adore Hemingway with an intensity unparalleled perhaps only by Tagore. Since Hemingway's death in 1961, slowly but steadily, Ernest Hemingway has become an icon to millions of Indian readers.

Hemingway has become so much a part of Indian culture and tradition that the provincial government of West Bengal commemorated the entire December 16, 1999 issue of *West Bengal: A West Bengal Government English Fortnightly* to the hundredth anniversary of Hemingway's birth. In the Foreword, the editors note, "This volume is not meant for introducing Hemingway to the readers of West Bengal. This is our humble tribute to the Master on the occasion of his birth centenary."[2] The editors could not be more accurate in saying that the people of West Bengal do not need an introduction to Hemingway. He is well-known to the vast majority of people across the Indian subcontinent—his picture needs no identifying caption.

The Indian reception of Hemingway may best be summed up by Dr. Somdatta Mandal, professor of English at Visva Bharati University in Santiniketan, West Bengal. According to Mandal, Hemingway's worldview can be readily assimilated by Hindu philosophical traditions:

> The Indian critical response to Ernest Hemingway is unique. The writer is appreciated for his depiction of rugged outdoor life, full of action and violence. The settings of his stories again provide the armchair traveler a window of the world. The exotic locations of Pamplona, Italian warfront, Africa, Constantinople, Michigan, Cuba, Paris or elsewhere, all add to this appeal. As a true supporter of democratic causes, his involvement in the Spanish Civil War against the Fascist forces is a praiseworthy characteristic, too. But what is more significant is the affinity that Indian readers find with Hemingway's worldview and that endorsed by our oriental

philosophy. Santiago's stoical endurance is exactly what the Bhagawat Gita preaches. Even Robert Jordan's suicide mission is interpreted according to the law of 'karma' endorsed by the scriptures. The 'code hero'/'apprentice hero' relationship is in tune with the 'guru/sishya' tradition. Further, in a traditional patriarchal society like ours, the male chauvinist hero and his masquerades are fully justified in all his actions, where issues like androgyny (like that depicted in "The Garden of Eden") are dismissed as temporary aberrations. How we have Indianized 'Papa' is clearly evident from the kind of articles written upon him by Indian scholars.[3]

Beyond this, and in the broadest sense of cultural synthesis, Hemingway has become an honorary citizen-author of postwar Bangladesh and India. As Mandal goes on to say,

> How far Hemingway is popular in this part of the world also becomes clear from another interesting phenomenon. Among the several 'special' Hemingway issues of magazines and journals published to commemorate his birth centennial, at least three are state-sponsored journals and as West Bengal has been under Marxist rule for the last twenty-three years, with a lot of anti-capitalistic issues on its agenda, it is no mean achievement. Ernest Hemingway has enabled scholars like us to explore avenues for a true cultural synthesis.[4]

For in the aftermath of their wars and struggles for independence, Hemingway's readers in Bangladesh and India continue to discover both in themselves and for themselves the nobility reflected in his ordinary heroes and code heroes from afar. His readers find an opening in his short stores and novels, one that—in the words of the Nobel Laureate Rabindranath Tagore—"has brought the distant near, and has made a stranger a brother."[5]

This celebratory encounter of reading Hemingway in Bangladesh and India not only demonstrates the continuing resonance of Hemingway's literary works but also challenges us to break through our own critical frames of reference in reading literature across the divides of geography, history and culture. Indeed, through his literary imagination and powers, Hemingway's literary legacy makes it possible for us—his readers—to discover a synthesis of his heroes and code heroes. Like the bridges that Hemingway's heroes encounter, it is a bridge to a fuller understanding of ourselves.

Notes

Introduction

1. D. S. R. Welland, "Hemingway's English Reputation," in *The Literary Reputation of Hemingway in Europe,* ed. Roger Asselineau (New York: New York University Press, 1965), 31.
2. Welland, 32.
3. Wyndham Lewis, quoted in Welland, 32.
4. Welland, 32.
5. Welland, 32.
6. Welland, 33.
7. Philip Henderson, quoted in Welland, 33.
8. Cyril Connolly, quoted in Welland, 34. The term *dogginess* is the British equivalent of *doggedness* in American usage.
9. V. S. Pritchett, quoted in Welland, 35.

Chapter One: Teaching American Literature in Bangladesh and India

1. Syed Manzoorul Islam, "Teaching American Literature in Bangladesh," *The Independent*, June 1, 2002, 2. (Internet Edition, accessed June 2, 2002.)
2. Syed Manzoorul Islam, 2.
3. Syed Manzoorul Islam, 1.
4. Syed Manzoorul Islam, 1.
5. Syed Manzoorul Islam, 1.
6. Syed Manzoorul Islam, 1.
7. North South University Syllabus: M.A. in Literature, 7-8.
8. University of Dhaka Syllabus: M.A. in Literature, 7-8.
9. Syed Manzoorul Islam, 2.
10. Golam Sarwar Chowdhury, interview by Ron Chepesiuk, *The Daily Star*, December 19, 2004, 1. (Internet Edition, accessed December 20, 2004.)
11. Golam Sarwar Chowdhury, 1.
12. Golam Sarwar Chowdhury, 1.
13. Golam Sarwar Chowdhury, 1.
14. Golam Sarwar Chowdhury, 1.
15. Golam Sarwar Chowdhury, 2.
16. Golam Sarwar Chowdhury, 2.
17. Syed Manzoorul Islam, 3.
18. Syed Manzoorul Islam, 3.
19. Golam Sarwar Chowdhury, 3.

20.   Golam Sarwar Chowdhury, 3.
21.   Golam Sarwar Chowdhury, 4.
22.   Golam Sarwar Chowdhury, 4.
23.   Syed Manzoorul Islam, 2.

Chapter Two: Hemingway's Legend in Bangladesh and India

1.   John A. Jones, "The Critics and the Public Legend," *Western Humanities Review* XIII (Autumn 1959): 387.
2.   Ernest Hemingway, *Death in the Afternoon* (New York: Charles Scribner's Sons, 1932), 191.
3.   Jones, 387-90.
4.   Clifton Fadiman, quoted in Jones, 390.
5.   Clifton Fadiman, "Ernest Hemingway: An American Byron" *Nation*, January 18, 1933, 63-64.
6.   Fadiman, 64.
7.   Fadiman, 64.
8.   Jones, 392.
9.   Jones, 393.
10.   Jones, 392-94.
11.   Malcolm Cowley, quoted in Jones, 397.
12.   Jones, 397.
13.   Tabassum Zaman, interview with Rabiul Hasan, June 16, 2004.
14.   Fakrul Alam, interview with Rabiul Hasan, May 24, 2004.
15.   Hasan Al Zayed, interview with Rabiul Hasan, May 24, 2004.
16.   Rebecca Sultana, interview with Rabiul Hasan, June 11, 2004.
17.   Khaliquzzaman Elias, interview with Rabiul Hasan, June 2, 2004.
18.   Tahmina Ahmed, interview with Rabiul Hasan, May 22, 2004.
19.   Showkat Hussain, interview with Rabiul Hasan, June 6, 2004.
20.   Kaiser Haque, interview with Rabiul Hasan, June 5, 2004.
21.   Shuchi Karim, interview with Rabiul Hasan, June 8, 2004.
22.   Sirajul Islam Chowdhury, interview with Rabiul Hasan, May 31, 2004.
23.   Khondker Ali Ashraf, interview with Rabiul Hasan, May 29, 2004.
24.   Tahmina Zaman Godhuli, interview with Rabiul Hasan, June 4, 2004.
25.   Zakeria Shirazii, "Ernest Hemingway: Artist of the Lost Generation," *The Independent*, November 13, 2004, 2.
26.   Carl Bloom, interview with Rabiul Hasan, May 30, 2004.
27.   Mansura Mahmuda Munni, interview with Rabiul Hasan, June 9, 2004.
28.   Tawhid Shams Chowdhury, interview with Rabiul Hasan, June 1, 2004.
29.   Philip Young, *Ernest Hemingway: A Reconsideration*. (University Park, PA: The Pennsylvania State University Press, 1966), 46.

Chapter Three: Hemingway's Short Stories in Bangladesh

1.   Shahida Sultana, interview with Rabiul Hasan, June 12-14, 2004.
2.   Sayma Arju, interview with Rabiul Hasan, May 28, 2004.
3.   Shahida Sultana, June 12-14, 2004.
4.   Shahida Sultana, June 12-14, 2004.
5.   Sayma Arju, May 28, 2004.
6.   Shahida Sultana, June 12-14, 2004.

7. Sayma Arju, May 28, 2004.
8. Shahida Sultana, June 12-14, 2004.
9. Sayma Arju, May 28, 2004.
10. Shahida Sultana, June 12-14, 2004.
11. Sayma Arju, May 28, 2004.
12. Tahsina Yasmin, interview with Rabiul Hasan, June 15, 2004.
13. Resalath Sultana, interview with Rabiul Hasan, June 11, 2004.
14. Resalath Sultana, June 11, 2004.
15. Shahida Sultana, June 12-14, 2004.
16. Shahida Sultana, June 12-14, 2004.
17. Shahida Sultana, June 12-14, 2004.
18. Resalath Sultana, June 11, 2004.
19. Shahida Sultana, June 12-14, 2004; Sayma Arju, May 28, 2004; Resalath Sultana, June 11, 2004; Tahsina Yasmin, June 15, 2004.
20. Shahida Sultana, June 12-14, 2004.
21. Frank O'Connor, *The Lonely Voice: A Study of the Short Story* (Cleveland: The World Publishing Company, 1962), 165.
22. Zerin Alam, interview with Rabiul Hasan, May 23, 2004.
23. Tahmina Ahmed, May 22, 2004.
24. Tahmina Ahmed, May 22, 2004.
25. Syed Shamsul Haque, "Firay Ashay" (One Who Returns), in *The Complete Stories of Syed Shamsul Haque.* (Dhaka, Bangladesh: Ananya, 2001), 80.
26. Kaiser Haque, June 5, 2004; Shahida Sultana, June 12-14, 2004.
27. Kaiser Haque, June 5, 2004.
28. Kaiser Haque, June 5, 2004; Shahida Sultana, June 12-14, 2004.

Chapter Four: Hemingway's Short Stories in India

1. Philip Young, 46.
2. Ernest Hemmingway, *A Moveable Feast* (Harmondsworth, Middlesex: Penguin Books, 1966), 15.
3. Syed Ali Hamid, *The Short Fiction of Ernest Hemingway: A Study in Major Themes* (New Delhi: Ashish Publishing House, 1985), 4.
4. Ernest Hemmingway, *A Moveable Feast* (1966), 15.
5. Carlos Baker, *Hemingway: The Writer as Artist* (Princeton: Princeton University Press, 1972), 117.
6. Syed Ali Hamid, 4.
7. Syed Ali Hamid, 12.
8. Syed Ali Hamid, 13.
9. Syed Ali Hamid, 13.
10. Syed Ali Hamid, 14.
11. Syed Ali Hamid, 15.
12. Syed Ali Hamid, 16.
13. Syed Ali Hamid, 25-26.
14. Syed Ali Hamid, 26.
15. Ernest Hemingway, *The Short Stories of Ernest Hemingway.* New York: Charles Scribner's Sons, 1954, quoted in Syed Ali Hamid, 26.
16. Ernest Hemingway, *The Short Stories of Ernest Hemingway,* quoted in Syed Ali Hamid, 26.
17. Syed Ali Hamid, 27.

18. Ernest Hemingway, "A Natural History of the Dead," quoted in Syed Ali Hamid, 27.
19. Ernest Hemingway, "A Natural History of the Dead," quoted in Syed Ali Hamid, 28.
20. Syed Ali Hamid, 28.
21. Ernest Hemingway, "A Natural History of the Dead," quoted in Syed Ali Hamid, 28.
22. Ernest Hemingway, "A Natural History of the Dead," quoted in Syed Ali Hamid, 28.
23. Syed Ali Hamid, 28.
24. N. Ramachandran Nair, *The Hemingway Arc* (Delhi: Pencraft International, 1994), 81.
25. Syed Ali Hamid, 30.
26. Ernest Hemingway, "The Butterfly and the Tank," quoted in Syed Ali Hamid, 30.
27. Syed Ali Hamid, 30-31.
28. Ernest Hemingway, ""A Way You'll Never Be," quoted in Syed Ali Hamid, 32.
29. Ernest Hemingway, "A Way You'll Never Be," quoted in Syed Ali Hamid, 32.
30. Syed Ali Hamid, 32.
31. N. Ramachandran Nair, 98.
32. Ernest Hemingway, ""Now I Lay Me," quoted in Syed Ali Hamid, 33.
33. N. Ramachandran Nair, 108.
34. Syed Ali Hamid, 33.
35. N. Ramachandran Nair, 40.
36. Syed Ali Hamid, 35.
37. Syed Ali Hamid, 35.
38. Ernest Hemingway, "Under the Ridge," quoted in Syed Ali Hamid, 36.
39. Syed Ali Hamid, 37.
40. Syed Ali Hamid, 37-38.
41. Syed Ali Hamid, 45.
42. Ernest Hemingway, "Soldier's Home," quoted in Syed Ali Hamid, 48.
43. Syed Ali Hamid, 50.
44. Syed Ali Hamid, 52.
45. Syed Ali Hamid, 53.
46. Syed Ali Hamid, 56.
47. Syed Ali Hamid, 56-57.
48. Syed Ali Hamid, 61.
49. Margaret Mitchell, *Gone with the Wind* (New York: Warner Books, 1993), 1024.
50. Syed Ali Hamid, 69.
51. Syed Ali Hamid, 70.
52. Syed Ali Hamid, 71-72.
53. Syed Ali Hamid, 73-74.
54. Syed Ali Hamid, 79.
55. Syed Ali Hamid, 80.
56. Syed Ali Hamid, 86-87.
57. Syed Ali Hamid, 95.
58. Syed Ali Hamid, 97.
59. Syed Ali Hamid, 104.
60. Syed Ali Hamid, 107.
61. Syed Ali Hamid, 111.

Chapter Five: Hemingway's Novels in Bangladesh

1. Kaiser Haque, June 5, 2004.
2. Kaiser Haque, June 5, 2004.
3. Farzana Akhter, interview with Rabiul Hasan, May 22, 2004.
4. Masrufa Ayesha Nusrat, interview with Rabiul Hasan, June 10, 2004.
5. Mohammad Tasmin Chowdhury, interview with Rabiul Hasan, May 31, 2004.
6. Golam Gaus Al-Quader, interview with Rabiul Hasan, May 25, 2004.
7. Nusrat Jahan, interview with Rabiul Hasan, June 7, 2004.
8. Tahmina Ahmed, May 22, 2004.
9. Firdous Azim, interview with Rabiul Hasan, May 29, 2004.
10. Shuchi Karim, June 8, 2004.
11. Tabassum Zaman, June 16, 2004.
12. Sirajul Islam Chowdhury, May 31, 2004.
13. Fakrul Alam, May 24, 2004.
14. Selim Sarwar, interview with Rabiul Hasan, June 10, 2004.
15. Zobaida Nasreen, interview with Rabiul Hasan, June 10, 2004.
16. Farzana Zebeen Khan, interview with Rabiul Hasan, June 8, 2004.
17. Kaiser Haque, "The Hemingway Code," *The Dhaka University Studies* XXVII, Part A (1977): 82.
18. Kaiser Haque, "The Hemingway Code," 82-86.
19. Zerin Alam, "Two Jazz Age Novels," *The Dhaka University Studies* (June 2000): 72.
20. Zerin Alam, "Two Jazz Age Novels," 72-74.
21. Zerin Alam, "Two Jazz Age Novels," 75.
22. Khaliquzzaman Elias, June 2, 2004.
23. Sirajul Islam Chowdhury, May 31, 2004.
24. Kaiser Haque, June 5, 2004.
25. Fakrul Alam, May 24, 2004.
26. Deena Forkan, interview with Rabiul Hasan, June 3, 2004.
27. Tahsina Yasmin, June 15, 2004.
28. Selim Sarwar, June 10, 2004.
29. Mohammad Tasmin Chowdhury, May 31, 2004.
30. Resalath Sultana, June 11, 2004.
31. Tahmina Ahmed, May 22, 2004.
32. Shuchi Karim, June 8, 2004.
33. Imrana Islam, interview with Rabiul Hasan, June 6, 2004.
34. Khaliquzzaman Elias, June 2, 2004.
35. Kaiser Haque, June 5, 2004.
36. Deena Forkan, June 3, 2004.
37. Selim Sarwar, June 10, 2004.
38. Sirajul Islam Chowdhury, May 31, 2004.
39. Ernest Hemingway to F. Scott Fitzgerald, December 15, 1925, quoted in Tahmina Ahmed, "War: Division Within and Without in *For Whom the Bell Tolls*," in *Hemingway: A Centennial Tribute*, ed. Niaz Zaman and Rebecca Haque (Dhaka, Bangladesh: University of Dhaka: 2007), 1-7.
40. Excerpt from John Donne's *Sermons*, quoted in Tahmina Ahmed, "War," 1-2.
41. Jeffrey Walsh, quoted in Tahmina Ahmed, "War," 2.
42. Ernest Hemingway, *For Whom the Bell* Tolls, quoted in Tahmina Ahmed, "War," 3-5.

43. Ernest Hemingway, *For Whom the Bell* Tolls, quoted in Tahmina Ahmed, "War," 5-7.
44. Deena Forkan, June 3, 2004.
45. Ernest Hemingway, *The Old Man and the Sea* (New York: Macmillan Publishing Company, 1986): 103.
46. Khaliquzzaman Elias, June 2, 2004.
47. Tahmina Zaman Godhuli, June 4, 2004.
48. Tahsina Yasmin, June 15, 2004.
49. Sirajul Islam Chowdhury, May 31, 2004.
50. Firdous Azim, May 29, 2004.
51. Farhana Yasmin Jahan, interview with Rabiul Hasan, June 7, 2004.
52. Tahmina Ahmed, May 22, 2004.
53. Farzana Zebeen Khan, June 8, 2004.
54. Nusrat Jahan, June 7, 2004.
55. Masrufa Ayesha Nusrat, June 10, 2004.
56. Selim Sarwar, June 10, 2004.
57. Ernest Hemingway, *The Old Man and the Sea,* trans. Ahmad Mazhar (Dhaka, Bangladesh: Student Ways, 1996): 5. Translator's Bengali Foreword translated by Rabiul Hasan.
58. Ernest Hemingway, *The Old Man and the Sea,* trans. Raoshan Jamil (Dhaka, Bangladesh: Projapoti Prokashan, 1987): 8. Translator's Bengali commentary translated by Rabiul Hasan.
59. Ernest Hemingway, *The Old Man and the Sea,* trans. Raoshan Jamil (Dhaka, Bangladesh: Projapoti Prokashan, 1987): 9. Translator's Bengali commentary translated by Rabiul Hasan.
60. Shuchi Karim, June 8, 2004.
61. Sayma Arju, May 28, 2004.

Chapter Six: Hemingway's Novels in India

1. Eccles. 1: 4.
2. Bhim S. Dahiya, *Hemingway's The Sun Also Rises: A Critical Introduction* (New Delhi: Lakeside Publishers, 1986): 15.
3. Bhim S. Dahiya, 18.
4. Eccles. 1: 15.
5. Bhim S. Dahiya, 18-19.
6. Ernest Hemingway, *The Sun Also Rises* (New York: Charles Scribner's Sons, 1926): 11.
7. Ernest Hemingway, *The Sun Also Rises*, 11.
8. Bhim S. Dahiya, 20.
9. Ernest Hemingway, *The Sun Also Rises*, 222.
10. Bhim S. Dahiya, 22.
11. Bhim S. Dahiya, 23-24.
12. Bhim S. Dahiya, 24-25.
13. Ernest Hemingway, *The Sun Also Rises*, 56.
14. Bhim S. Dahiya, 29-30.
15. Bhim S. Dahiya, 31-32.
16. Bhim S. Dahiya, 37-38.
17. Bhim S. Dahiya, 72-73.
18. Ernest Hemingway, *The Sun Also Rises*, 3-4.

19. Bhim S. Dahiya, 74-75.
20. Ernest Hemingway, *The Sun Also Rises*, 60-61.
21. Bhim S. Dahiya, 78-79.
22. Bhim S. Dahiya, 83-84.
23. Ernest Hemingway, *The Sun Also Rises*, 240-41.
24. Ramji Lall, *A Farwell to Arms: A Critical Study* (New Delhi: Rama Brothers, 2001): 4.
25. Ramji Lall, 14.
26. Arindam Dasgupta, interview with Rabiul Hasan, June 24, 2005.
27. Indranil Mitra, interview with Rabiul Hasan, June 24, 2005.
28. Sayantan Dasgupta, interview with Rabiul Hasan, June 24, 2005.
29. Sobha Chattopadhya, interview with Rabiul Hasan, June 24, 2005.
30. Uma K. Alladi, "Existentialism in the Novels of Hemingway and Camus," *The Literary Half-Yearly* 21, no. 2 (1980): 45.
31. Satyabrata Das, *Ernest Hemingway: The Turning Point* (New Delhi: Atlantic Publishers and Distributors, 1996): 21.
32. J. P. Tripathi, *Ernest Hemingway: A Study in His Evolution*. Bareilly (Uttar Pradesh: Prakash Book Depot, 1990): 422.
33. Sanjukta Dasgupta, *The Novels of Huxley and Hemingway: A Study of Two Planes of Reality* (New Delhi: Prestige Books, 1996): 82.
34. Sanjukta Dasgupta, 84.
35. Sanjukta Dasgupta, 85.
36. Sanjukta Dasgupta, 85-86.
37. S. S. Sangwan and Satyapal Dahiya, "Hemingway's Humanist Outlook: A Study of *A Farewell to Arms*," *Punjab University Research Bulletin (Arts)* 21, no. 1 (April 1990): 55.
38. S. S. Sangwan and Satyapal Dahiya, 55.
39. S. S. Sangwan and Satyapal Dahiya, 58-59.
40. S. S. Sangwan and Satyapal Dahiya, 59.
41. S. S. Sangwan and Satyapal Dahiya, 60.
42. S. S. Sangwan and Satyapal Dahiya, 61-62.
43. S. S. Sangwan and Satyapal Dahiya, 61.
44. Aparajita Nanda, "Gender Crisis, Androgyny and the Length of Hair: A Look at *For Whom the Bell Tolls, A Moveable Feast* and 'The Garden of Eden,'" *Journal of the Department of English, Rabindra Bharati University* V (1998-99): 107.
45. Aparajita Nanda, "Hemingway's Search for Identity—from *The Sun Also Rises, A Farewell to Arms, For Whom the Bell Tolls* to 'The Garden of Eden'," *West Bengal: A West Bengal Government English Fortnightly* XLI, no. 23 (December 16, 1999): 157.
46. Aparajita Nanda, 158.
47. Aparajita Nanda, 158-59.
48. Aparajita Nanda, 158.
49. Aparajita Nanda, 157.
50. Ramesh Kumar Srivastava, *Determinism in Hemingway* (Amritsar: Guru Nanak Dev University, 1975): 41.
51. Ramji Lall, 16.
52. Ramji Lall, 16-17.
53. Ramesh Kumar Srivastava, 42-43.
54. Ernest Hemingway, *Death in the Afternoon* (New York: Charles Scribner's Sons, 1932): 192.
55. Ramesh Kumar Srivastava, 43.

56.   Ramesh Kumar Srivastava, 50.
57.   Ramesh Kumar Srivastava, 46.
58.   Ramesh Kumar Srivastava, 47.
59.   Ramesh Kumar Srivastava, 48.
60.   Ramesh Kumar Srivastava, 49.
61.   Ramesh Kumar Srivastava, 49.
62.   Ramesh Kumar Srivastava, 50.
63.   Ernest Hemingway, *For Whom the Bell Tolls* (New York: Charles Scribner's Sons, 1940): 467.
64.   Ramesh Kumar Srivastava, 51.
65.   Ramesh Kumar Srivastava, 52.
66.   Ramesh Kumar Srivastava, 52-53.
67.   Ramesh Kumar Srivastava, 88
68.   T. R. Henn, *The Harvest of Tragedy* (London: Methuen, 1966): 27-28.
69.   Ramesh Kumar Srivastava, 89-90.
70.   Aristotle, *Poetics*, trans. Preston H. Epps (Chapel Hill: University of North Carolina Press, 1942): 20.
71.   Ramesh Kumar Srivastava, 90-91.
72.   Lionel Trilling, "An American in Spain," *Partisan Review,* 8 (1941): 64.
73.   Ramesh Kumar Srivastava, 91.
74   Ramesh Kumar Srivastava, 99.
75.   Aristotle, 24.
76.   Ramesh Kumar Srivastava, 99-100.
77.   Ernest Hemingway, 164.
78.   Ramesh Kumar Srivastava, 101.
79.   Ramesh Kumar Srivastava, 101-2.
80.   Ernest Hemingway, 467.
81.   S. C. Mundra, *Hemingway's The Old Man and the Sea.* (Bareilly, Uttar Pradesh: Prakash Book Depot, 1977): 25.
82.   Sobha Chattopadhya, interview with Rabiul Hasan, June 24, 2005.
83.   Sanjukta Dasgupta, 81.
84.   Sanjukta Dasgupta, 119.
85.   Uma K. Alladi, 44.
86.   Uma K. Alladi, 44-45.
87.   Murari Prasad, "The Sea as Symbol in *The Old Man and the Sea,*" *Indian Journal of American Studies* 22, no. 2 (Summer 1992): 89.
88.   Murari Prasad, 89-90.
89.   Murari Prasad, 93.
90.   Murari Prasad, 95.
91.   J. P. Tripathi, 426.
92.   N. Ramachandran Nair, 75.
93.   Subhas Sarkar, "A Modernist Quest for Martyrdom: Hemingway's *The Old Man and the Sea* and T. S. Eliot's *Murder in the Cathedral,*" *West Bengal XLI, no. 23* (December 16, 1999): 67.
94.   Subhas Sarkar, 68.
95.   Ernest Hemingway, *The Old Man and the Sea*, quoted in Sarkar, 69.
96.   Subhas Sarkar, 68.
97.   Subhas Sarkar, 70.
98.   Subhas Sarkar, 70.
99.   Subhas Sarkar, 70.
100. Ernest Hemingway, *The Old Man and the Sea*, quoted in Sarkar, 103.

101. Satyanarain Singh, "The Psychology of Heroic Living in *The Old Man and the Sea*," *Osmania Journal of English Studies* 9, no. 1 (1972): 7.
102. Ernest Hemingway, quoted in Abraham H. Lass, ed., *A Student Guide to 50 American Novels*, 4th ed. (New York: Washington Square Press, 1967), 174.
103. Abraham H. Lass, p. 174.
104. Satyanarain Singh, 8.
105. Satyanarain Singh, 9.
106. Satyanarain Singh, 14.
107. Ramji Lall, 59.
108. Lisa Tyler, *Student Companion to Ernest Hemingway* (Westport, CT: Greenwood Press, 2001), 29.
109. Ramji Lall, *The Old Man and the Sea* (New Delhi: Rama Brothers, 2001): 56.
110. Ramji Lall, 58.

Conclusion

1. Hasan Azizul Haque, *The Daily Prothom Alo*, 15.
2. Satinath Ray, "Editor's Foreword," *West Bengal: A West Bengal Government English Fortnightly* XLI, no. 23 (December 16, 1999): 4.
3. Somdatta Mandal, "The Indian Critical Reception of Ernest Hemingway: A Bibliographical Overview" in *The Ernest Hemingway Companion,* ed. Somdatta Mandal. (Kolkata, West Bengal: SAS Enterprise, 2002), 274-75.
4. Mandal, 275.
5. Rabindranath Tagore, Acceptance Telegram from Rabindranath Tagore read at the Nobel Banquet, Stockholm, December 10, 1913, in *Nobel Lectures, Literature 1901-1967*, ed. Horst Frenz (New York: Elsevier Publishing Co. 1969), 133.

Bibliography

Books

Ahmed, Tahmina. "War: Division Within and Without in *For Whom the Bell Tolls.*" In *Hemingway: A Centennial Tribute*, edited by Niaz Zaman and Rebecca Haque, 1-7. Dhaka, Bangladesh: University of Dhaka, 2007.

Alladi, Uma K. "Hemingway: The Quintessential American?" In *Ernest Hemingway: Centennial Essays*, edited by E. Nageswara Rao, 26-30. Delhi: Pencraft International, 2000.

Aristotle. *Poetics.* Translated by Preston H. Epps. Chapel Hill: University of North Carolina Press, 1942.

Baker, Carlos. *A Life Story.* New York: Bantam Books, 1970.

———. *Hemingway: The Writer as Artist.* Princeton: Princeton University Press, 1972.

Dahiya, Bhim S. *Hemingway's A Farewell to Arms: A Critical Study.* Delhi: Academic Foundation, 1992.

———. *Hemingway's The Sun Also Rises: A Critical Introduction.* New Delhi: Lakeside Publishers, 1986.

———. *Hero in Hemingway: Study in Development.* New Delhi: Bahri Publications, 1978.

Das, Satyabrata. *Ernest Hemingway: The Turning Point.* New Delhi: Atlantic Publishers and Distributors, 1996.

———. "From the Bullring into Politics: A Study of Hemingway's Changing Response." In *Literature and Politics in Twentieth-Century America*, edited by J. L. Plakkoottam and Prashant Sinha, 99-105. Hyderabad: American Studies Research Center, 1993.

Dasgupta, Sanjukta. "The Crack-Up: Scott Fitzgerald, Ernest Hemingway and the Lost Generation." In *F. Scott Fitzgerald: A Centennial Tribute*, vol.1, edited by Somdatta Mandal, 30-38. London: Sangam Books, 1998.

———. *The Novels of Huxley and Hemingway: A Study of Two Planes of Reality.* New Delhi: Prestige Books, 1996.

Frenz, Horst, ed. *Nobel Lectures, Literature 1901–1967.* New York: Elsevier Publishing Co., 1969.

Hamid, Syed Ali. *The Short Fiction of Ernest Hemingway: A Study in Major Themes.* New Delhi: Ashish Publishing House, 1985.

Haque, Syed Shamsul. "Firay Ashay" (One Who Returns). In *The Complete Stories of Syed Shamsul Haque*, 80. Dhaka, Bangladesh: Ananya, 2001.

Henn, T. R. *The Harvest of Tragedy.* London: Methuen, 1966.

Jain, Satya Prakash. *Hemingway: A Study of His Short Stories.* New Delhi: Arnold Heinemann, 1985.

Josh, S. "Foregrounding the Sea: A Reading of Hemingway's *The Old Man and the Sea* and Thakazhi's *Chemmeen*." In *Ernest Hemingway: Centennial Essays*, edited by E. Nageswara Rao, 71-77. Delhi: Pencraft International, 2000.

Lall, Ramji. *A Farwell to Arms: A Critical Study*. New Delhi: Rama Brothers, 2001.

Lass, Abraham H., ed. *A Student Guide to 50 American Novels*, 4th ed. New York: Washington Square Press, 1967.

Mandal, Somdatta. "The Indian Critical Reception of Ernest Hemingway: A Bibliographical Overview." In *The Ernest Hemingway Companion*, edited by Somdatta Mandal, 274-75, Kolkata, West Bengal: SAS Enterprise, 2002.

Mitchell, Margaret. *Gone with the Wind*. New York: Warner Books, 1993.

Mundra, S. C. *Ernest Hemingway: Novelist*. Bareilly, Uttar Pradesh: Prakash Book Depot, 1972.

———. *Ernest Hemingway: The Impact of War on His Life and Works*. Bareilly, Uttar Pradesh: Prakash Book Depot, 1988.

Nair, N. Ramachandran. "Re-Emergence of the Artist in "The Snows of Kilimanjaro."" In *Ernest Hemingway: Centennial Essays*, edited by E. Nageswara Rao, 90-98. Delhi: Pencraft International, 2000.

———. *The Hemingway Arc*. Delhi: Pencraft International, 1994.

O'Connor, Frank. *The Lonely Voice: A Study of the Short Story*. Cleveland: The World Publishing Company, 1962.

Paul, Sukrita. *Man, Woman and Androgyny: Study of the Novels of Theodore Dreiser, Scott Fitzgerald, and Ernest Hemingway*. New Delhi: Indus Publishing Company, 1989.

Singh, Aviram. "Threshold Angel and War: Three Case Studies of Heroines from American Fiction." In *Ernest Hemingway: Centennial Essays*, edited by E. Nageswara Rao, 46-53. Delhi: Pencraft International, 2000.

Srivastava, Ramesh Kumar. *Determinism in Hemingway*. Amritsar: Guru Nanak Dev University, 1975.

———. *Hemingway and His For Whom the Bell Tolls*. Amritsar: Guru Nanak Dev University, 1980.

Tripathi, J. P. *Ernest Hemingway: A Study in His Evolution*. Bareilly, Uttar Pradesh: Prakash Book Depot, 1990.

Tyler, Lisa. *Student Companion to Ernest Hemingway*. Westport, CT: Greenwood Press, 2001.

Welland, D. S. R. "Hemingway's English Reputation." In *The Literary Reputation of Hemingway in Europe*, edited by Roger Asselineau, 31-33. New York: New York University Press, 1965.

Young, Philip. *Ernest Hemingway: A Reconsideration*. University Park, PA: Pennsylvania State University Press, 1966.

Articles

"An American Story Teller." *Time* LXIV (1954): 72.

Alam, Zerin. "Two Jazz Age Novels." *Dhaka University Studies* (June 2000): 71-75.

Alladi, Uma K. "Existentialism in the Novels of Hemingway and Camus." *The Literary Half-Yearly*, 21, no. 2 (1980): 44-45.

Cowley, Malcolm. "A Portrait of Mister Papa." *Life,* January 10, 1949, 87-101.

Dasgupta, Sanjukta. "A Writer Is Like a Gypsy:' Hemingway and Politics." *West Bengal: A West Bengal Government English Fortnightly* XLI, no. 23 (December 16, 1999): 13-22.

————. "Huck and Nick: Mark Twain and Ernest Hemingway's Bohemians." *Journal of the Department of English, Rabindra Bharati University* V (1998-99): 53-63.

————. "Rape of Spain: Ernest Hemingway's Ideology." *Journal of the Department of English, University of Calcutta* XXVI, no. 1 (1998-99): 15-24.

Fadiman, Clifton. "Ernest Hemingway: An American Byron," *Nation*, January 18, 1933.

Haldar, Indrani. "Between Cezanne and Picasso: Hemingway's Artistic Inheritance." *West Bengal: A West Bengal Government English Fortnightly* XLI, no. 23 (December 16, 1999): 23-32.

————. "Hemingway's In Our Time: The Writer's Continuing Relevance." *Journal of the Department of English, Rabindra Bharati University* V (1998-99): 11-19.

————. "Picasso, Hemingway and the Bull." *Indian Journal of American Studies* 16, no.1 (Winter 1996): 27-32.

Islam, Syed Manzoorul. "Teaching American Literature in Bangladesh." *The Independent*, June 1, 2002, 1-4.

Jain, Satya Prakash. "'Hills Like White Elephants:' A Study." *Indian Journal of American Studies* 1, no. 3 (July 1970): 33-38.

Jones, John A. "The Critics and the Public Legend." *Western Humanities Review* XIII (Autumn 1959): 387-410.

Kumar, Sukrita Paul. "Towards the New Woman: The Shifting of Sex Roles in Dreiser, Fitzgerald and Hemingway." *Indian Journal of American Studies* 17:1-2 (1987): 65-73.

Nanda, Aparajita. "Gender Crisis, Androgyny and the Length of Hair: A Look at *For Whom the Bell Tolls, A Moveable Feast* and 'The Garden of Eden'." *Journal of the Department of English, Rabindra Bharati University* V (1998-99): 107-114.

————. "Hemingway's Search for Identity—from *The Sun Also Rises, A Farewell to Arms, For Whom the Bell Tolls* to 'The Garden of Eden'." *West Bengal: A West Bengal Government English Fortnightly* XLI, no. 23 (December 16, 1999): 157-59.

Paul, Ajanta. "Hemingway's Short Fiction and the Problematics of Peregrination." *Journal of the Department of English, Rabindra Bharti University* V (1998-99): 120-25.

Prasad, Murari. "The Sea as Symbol in *The Old Man and the Sea*." *Indian Journal of American Studies* 22, no. 2 (Summer 1992): 89-95.

————. "The Sea as Symbol in The Old Man and the Sea." *Journal of the Department of English, Rabindra Bharati University* V (1998-99): 184-93.

Ray, Satinath. "Editor's Foreword." *West Bengal: A West Bengal Government English Fortnightly* XLI, no. 23 (December 16, 1999): 4.

Redman, Ben R. "The Champ and the Referees." *Saturday Review of Literature* XXXIII (October 28, 1950): 15-16, 38.

Sangwan, S. S. "Money and Morals in Hemingway's Short Stories." *Punjab University Research Bulletin* (Arts) 21, no. 2 (October 1990): 69-73.

————. "What Is American in American Literature: Ernest Hemingway: A Case Study." *West Bengal: A West Bengal Government English Fortnightly* XLI, no. 23 (December 16, 1999): 47-52.

Sangwan, S. S. and Dahiya, Satyapal. "Hemingway's Humanist Outlook: A Study of *A Farewell to Arms*." *Punjab University Research Bulletin* (Arts) 21, no. 1 (April 1990): 55-62.

Sarkar, Subhas. "A Modernist Quest for Martyrdom: Hemingway's *The Old Man and the Sea* and T. S. Eliot's *Murder in the Cathedral*." *West Bengal: A West Bengal Government English Fortnightly* XLI, no. 23 (December 16, 1999): 67-70.

Shirazii, Zakeria. "Ernest Hemingway: Artist of the Lost Generation." *The Independent*, November 13, 2004.

Singh, Satyanarain. "The Psychology of Heroic Living in *The Old Man and the Sea*." *Osmania Journal of English Studies* 9, no.1 (1972): 7-14.

Trilling, Lionel. "An American in Spain." *Partisan Review* 8 (1941): 64.

Works by Ernest Hemingway in English

Hemingway, Ernest. *A Farewell to Arms*. New York: Charles Scribner's Sons, 1929.

———. *A Moveable Feast*. Harmondsworth, Middlesex: Penguin Books, 1966.

———. *Death in the Afternoon*. New York: Charles Scribner's Sons, 1932.

———. *For Whom the Bell Tolls*. New York: Charles Scribner's Sons, 1940.

———. *Hemingway's A Farewell to Arms*. Bareilly, Uttar Pradesh: Prakash Book Depot, 1987.

———. *Hemingway's For Whom the Bell Tolls*. Bareilly, Uttar Pradesh: Prakash Book Depot, 1986.

———. *Hemingway's The Old Man and the Sea*. Bareilly, Uttar Pradesh: Prakash Book Depot, 1977.

———. *The Old Man and the Sea*. New Delhi: Rama Brothers, 2001.

———. *The Old Man and the Sea*. New York: Macmillan Publishing Company, 1986.

———. *The Short Stories of Ernest Hemingway*. New York: Charles Scribner's Sons, 1954.

———. *The Sun Also Rises*. New York: Charles Scribner's Sons, 1926.

Works by Ernest Hemingway in Bengali Translation

Hemingway, Ernest. *A Farewell to Arms*. Translated by Neaz Morshed. Dhaka, Bangladesh: Sheba Prokashani, 1988.

———. *A Farewell to Arms*. Translated by Qamrul Islam. Dhaka, Bangladesh: Mowla Brothers, 1970.

———. *Stories of Hemingway*. Translated by Kawsar Hussain. Dhaka, Bangladesh: Bangla Academy, 2004.

———. *The Fifth Column*. Translated by Sheikh Apala Hakim. Dhaka, Bangladesh: Sheba Prokashani, 2002.

———. *The Old Man and The Sea*. Translated by Ahmad Mazhar. Bangladesh: Student Ways, 1996.

———. *The Old Man and The Sea*. Translated by Raoshan Jamil. Dhaka, Bangladesh: Projapoti Prokashan, 1987.

———. *The Sun Also Rises*. Translated by Abul Fazl. Dhaka, Bangladesh: Mowla Brothers, 1974.

Miscellaneous Sources

Ahmed, Humayun. Television Plays.

North South University Syllabus. M. A. in Literature.

University of Dhaka Syllabus. M.A. in Literature.

Index

9/11. *See* September 11, 2001

abortion, 23-25, 43; dilemma of, 23-25; in Bangladesh, 23-24; *See also* parenthood
alcohol, 56, 72-73
American literature. *See* literature, American
American studies: debate over, ix, 6-9; funding of, 7-8; movement for, 5-6, 9; role of, 6; problems of, 8

BAAS. *See* Bangladesh Association for American Studies
Bangladesh: independence of, ix, xv, 2, 13, 17, 27, 47; libraries in, 2; prewar, ix, 11, 97; postwar, 57, 98; sources for research in, 11, 97; universities in, 1, 5, 6, 11, 13-14; *See also* culture, Bangladeshi; critics, Bangladeshi; Pakistan, East; war, between East and West Pakistan
Bangladesh Association for American Studies (BAAS), 6, 9
bias: cultural, 8; racial, 8; *See also* curricula, cultural bias of; multiculturalism
bridge: as metaphor, 34, 38, 58, 60, 81-88, 99; in titles, 33, 38, 39
British literature. *See* literature, British
British rule. *See* colonialism
Bush, George W., 7

Charter Act of 1813. *See* colonialism
civil war. *See* war, between East and West Pakistan
code hero, 51-52, 75, 89, 95, 99; cultural relevance of, 99; *See also* heroes; men; protagonists

colonialism: academy under, xiii, xv, 1; critique of, xiii; legacy of, xv, 1, 5
critics of Hemingway: attacks on, 12-13; attitudes of, 11; American, 12, 17; Bangladeshi, xv, 11, 13-15, 17-18, 27-28, 47-48, 50, 61, 65; British, xiii-xv; expatriate, 15; gender, 49, 53, 79-80; Indian, xv, 11, 17-18, 67-71, 81, 89-90, 92, 98-99; Marxist, 97; working definition of, x; *See also* Hemingway, legend; journalists; publishers
culture: American, xvi, 6, 9, 48; Bangladeshi, 6, 23, 25; Indian, 98; *See also* bias, cultural; Hemingway, cultural relevance of; multiculturalism
cultural synthesis. *See* Hemingway, cultural relevance of
curricula: English, xv, 2, 3-4; cultural bias of, 2, 8; *See also* literature, teaching of; bias; multiculturalism

epigraphs, 50, 57, 67
existentialism, 30-31, 43, 64, 77-78, 92, 93, 95; and war, 30, 38, 40, 53

films, 3, 9, 55, 63, 75, 89
freedom: individual, 15; loss of, 43; of religion, 6; personal, 42-44, 47, 79; *See also* philosophy; war

Hemingway, Ernest: biographies of, 17; cultural relevance of, 16, 19-20, 25-26, 29-30, 65, 97-99; death of, 14-17, 80, 98; influence of, xiv-xv, 28-29, 98; legend, 3, 11-16; literary importance of, xiii-xiv, xv, 27-28, 54; literary themes of, 12,

16, 25-27, 33, 47-50, 52, 55, 71;
     popularity of, xiii, 3, 28, 54, 80,
     89, 98-99; relation to readers, xiii;
     See also critics; heroes; code hero;
     lost generation
heroes: cultural relevance of, 16, 19-20,
     65, 99; depiction of, 16, 30, 62-65,
     71, 87-88, 94-95; empathy with,
     17, 28, 64-65; modern, 97;
     psychology of, 16, 89, 94;
     Shakespearean, 70, 87; *See also*
     code hero; men; protagonists
Hinduism: priests of, 47, 48, 50, 97
humor, 16, 51, 71-74

iceberg principle. *See* metaphor
India: Bengali-speaking provinces of,
     11; colonial, xiii, xv;
     independence of, xv, 11, 17;
     sources for research in, 11, 97;
     universities in, 1, 5, 11; *See also*
     critics, Indian
irony, 31, 35, 38-39, 51, 83-85;
     ultimate, 88
Islam, 23; and governance, 7; preachers
     of, 47, 48, 50, 56, 97; *See also*
     culture, Bangladeshi; religion

journals. *See* publishers, magazine
journalists, 13, 15; Hemingway as, 13,
     33; *See also* critics; publishers

literature: American, xiv, xv, xvi, 2;
     Bengali, 28, 29; British, xiv, 1, 27;
     modern, 2; study of, xiv; teaching
     of, xv, 1, 3-4, 5, 8, 9; world, xv;
     See also curricula
lost generation, 39, 47, 48-50, 52-53,
     61, 67-71, 97; *See also*
     Hemingway, themes of

marriage, 17, 23, 56; depiction of, 20-
     21, 22, 23
martyrdom, 89, 92-94; *See also*
     symbolism, Christian
men: as symbols 12, 46; old, 25, 38, 39,
     40, 62-65, 90, 92, 94-95; *See also*
     code heroes; heroes; protagonists
metaphor, 69, 82; *See also* bridge;
     philosophy, of life; symbolism;
     wound

movies. *See* films
mullahs. *See* Islam, preachers of
multiculturalism, 8, 9

National Endowment for the
     Humanities (NEH), 7; *See also*
     American studies, funding of
NEH. *See* National Endowment for the
     Humanities
newspapers. *See* publishers
Nobel Prize, xv, 14, 28, 99
novels: adaptations of, 3, 75, 89;
     American, xiv, 54; Bengali, 44;
     British, xiv, 73; context of, 34, 67,
     80-81; *See also* films

Pakistan: East, ix, xv, 2, 11; West, ix,
     xv; independence of, xv; *See*
     Bangladesh, prewar; *See also* war,
     between East and West Pakistan
parenthood, 43
periodicals. *See* publishers
philosophy:
     anti-war, 74-75, 81; of life, 26, 56,
     68-69; of liberal humanism, 78-
     79; oriental, 98-99; *See also*
     Hemingway, cultural relevance of;
     Hinduism
political consciousness, ix, 7, 26, 57,
     60, 86-87
protagonists: male, 43-44, 45; *See also*
     freedom; heroes; men
publishers, 11, 12, 14, 19, 99; Bengali,
     15, 19, 27, 47, 64; magazine, 12,
     13, 17, 99; newspaper, 15, 17; *See*
     also journalists; translations

racial bias. *See* bias
realism, 27, 28, 55-56, 60, 62, 75, 89
religion: and democracy, 6-7; and
     secularism, 6-7; fundamentalist, 6-
     7, 47-48, 97; *See also* critics,
     Bangladeshi; Islam; Hinduism,
     priests of
romanticism, 12, 34, 46, 54; as escape,
     68

sainthood, 89, 92, 94
satire. *See* humor
September 11, 2001, ix, x, 7, 8, 9

Shakespeare, William. *See* heroes,
    Shakespearean
short stories, 16, 19, 26-27, 29-30, 31,
    98; adaptations of, 3; phases of,
    32-33; themes of, 33-34, 38-39,
    43-44; *See also* translations
Spanish Civil War, 15, 33, 36, 56-57,
    62, 81-83, 85-87, 98; *See also*
    freedom
Stein, Gertrude. *See* lost generation
suffering. *See* war; wound
suicide, 14, 17, 25, 61, 99; and
    androgyny, 80; as analogous to
    war, 38; *See also* Hemingway,
    death of
symbolism, 30, 37-38, 40, 52, 53, 55,
    63, 70, 82-86, 91-92; and irony,
    83, 85; Bengali, 25; Christian, 38,
    89, 92, 94; *See also* bridge; irony;
    men; wound

Tagore, Rabindranath, 98, 99; *See also*
    literature, modern

translations, ix, 2-3, 9-10; and realism,
    60; of Hemingway's works, 17,
    19, 26-27, 30, 47, 54, 64, 98

United States Information Service
    (USIS), 2-3
USIS. *See* United States Information
    Service

war: between East and West Pakistan,
    ix, xv, 11, 47, 97; First World, 15,
    39, 49-50, 56; literary potential of,
    52, 57; *See also* existentialism,
    and war; Spanish Civil War;
    suicide, as analogous to war
wound, 17, 23, 40, 45, 50, 60, 75, 78;
    as symbol, 37, 84-87; psychic, 16,
    36-37, 53
World War I. *See* war, First World
West Bengal, 11, 98-99; Marxist rule
    of, 99

About the Author

A native of Bangladesh, and a naturalized U.S. citizen, Rabiul Hasan is a poet, fiction writer and translator of English and American literature. His short stories and poems have appeared in more than forty journals and anthologies published in the United States, Canada, and Malaysia. Hasan is the author of *Madonna of the Rain*, a collection of his poetry published in 2008 by the Rockford Writers' Guild Press. Currently, he is working on two full-length collections of poetry entitled, "Stars in the Darkness" and "Miriam." He is listed in *A Directory of American Poets and Fiction Writers*.

In addition to his publications in English, Hasan has published two books of his poetry and three books of his short stories in Bengali, and translated into Bengali the short stories and poems by a number of British and American authors including, Ernest Hemingway, Erskine Caldwell, Truman Capote, Stephen Crane, William Carlos Williams, D. H. Lawrence, John O'Hara, Cecil Day Lewis, John Collier, Brian Swann, and Langston Hughes.

Professor Hasan earned a PhD in English (American Literature) at Texas Tech University, and is an assistant professor of English at Southern University in Baton Rouge, Louisiana.

www.ingramcontent.com/pod-product-compliance
Lightning Source LLC
Chambersburg PA
CBHW030653110726
47901CB00002B/692